KNOW FISH

Book III

the navigators

Vincent Ferrini

The University of Connecticut Library

Storrs, Connecticut

Manufactured in the United States of America

Grateful acknowledgements to the editors of: Himma #4; the church press; The Gloucester Daily Times; AMERICA ONE; Black Rose; Arts Institute Journal; MAENAD; Red Hand Book II, Sapiens.

The play BASE-BALL was performed by Cape Ann Theatre the last of September and the first of October, 1983, at the Blackburn Tavern in Gloucester.

First Edition.

Library of Congress Cataloging in Publication Data

Ferrini, Vincent, 1913 -
Know fish.

I. Title.
PS3511.E7246K64 1984 811'.52 83-27508
ISBN 0-917590-08-2

Composition by Wang Laboratories, Inc.
Cover by the maker, assisted by Kate Boyle.

I wish to thank Patty Welch, Helen MacLeod Georgenis, Jain Tarnower, Gay Walley and Sheila F. Corman for their time and enthusiasm, and Buz Bever for her generosities and endurances.

Printed by: **Celecom Corporation**
East Longmeadow, Mass.

CONTENTS

TEN POUND LIGHT

ONE

- Primordium

A rock point of shifting athanasia
in a galaxy of fishes

Milkweed mistress mother wife beloved friend
the spume of the Moon

the Wingaersheek of our Solitudes
always a flesh of white sands
and a lineage of hot echoes
now proverbs

A
((as the Ocean
never seen two days)

B
When I first laid eyes on Thee & Thine
my heart's glow took in
cod, hake, flouder, mackerel heavens
dear granite glances, whippoorwill iris, branched
backbones
& adoring instincts

going in any direction
siphoning the lore
& returning it

Holy the hills, holy the sea
holy the air
all is Mana
& innocence spacing Time

seeing as gravemarkers
as canoes, bronzed faces do
with second sight the first is wrought of

I, a singing once inhabited
guiding galactic energies

C

As somewhere perhaps a fish eyed people
& this pilot for a continent
are the turners over,
Tlamatinimes

rare frequencies with nothing to lose
seizing the Language

against the Elite & their Elected
Flunkeys
undoing the 13 Houses))

D
The stain of Pluto is upon the air & sea
we are tales others hear
clearly

Look, the unity of MATTER

E
Indian power
is Here
stirring the stone sleepers

on the roads to the abalone Temple
one by Fishes
the other by Dreams

create yourself out of yourself
out of the oppressing polar deaths
this is the true work

actions from that emerging
straight to the Juggler Thee
O mix the chemicals of Imagination & History

the nodes of material existence
herein hide, uncover the facts
the thesaurus

calling what light flecks off that pedestal
always by a contrary
the focusing <u>pitchblende</u>

F
The raging Jehovah
hey, unexpected, how many cards?
None

In front
the Vacuum is a sucking
blastfurnace

Love is the Measurer of the Materials
night's load
                                                            speech

driven

                    as the other Root
& equally fired

TWO

bulletin

Live with me
but not in the same house
lay with me
but not in one room
engage me
but dont have any fixed notions
sup with me
but not at the same table

THREE

the weathervane

We are at the frontier of Love
the unsettled City

FOUR

news

Itineraries by silhouette
get thy bird functioning

these headstones have glinting eyes

who has not loved in a cemetery
& sung with the topmost limbs

the Eastern side has primaveras in it
the Western goes down
with glimpses of the momentary eternals
for paring delusions away

the gradations of gentle men
ah the shades

2 ladies and 2 gallants
tapping tall steel canes on the flat
arctic Ice Age

J Jensen at 40

things never seen before –
a territorial ghost time
& landing on a light

it was a sundown
Fitz Hugh Lane went wild on
because he couldn't be everyplace
at the same instant

how the levels change
we dont astound
one another
as much as any Amendment does!

as a conquered expansion is

by the hearing heart!

FIVE

the rumor from the House that isnt there

Fogs roll in on white cerebellums
in a junkshop a sea shell soul
the damp on the TIMES comes from that Santa
Maria's trap
the editor is the end of a bare cable
the photos breezing by the Lady of Extreme Unction
the Empire's still born signal
the Dogbar's lamp helps navigate the Night
the jugging through the canals of the Wax Museum
Winslow's winks
the air crosses of the 200 mile limit
goosing the Federal Monolith
as long as 'social' doesnt jump ship
we'll all be Hasids at the WELFARE
the trick of waylaying Fear is count yourself as
dead anyway
and then Live!

Fish the summers, fuck in the winter, & panhandle
the Floridas of the Soul

Forget the glued to the spider's prism
who have signed with their blood
Entrepreneur's Manifesto

The roofs are my retreats
mosques, turning cones, & private windmills
seen from stars directing dreamers

what house what view has burst its boundary
clusters on Aphrodite's rock
the uninterrupted intercourse cells and atoms
the spectra has intimations of
fearing to tap this unused inexhaustible generator

There are as many realities as there are creatures
& substances
the last pillages of our Birds of Prey
beneath the skin what animal is sacrificed

Go berserk, but dont make waves

The Angelus! the starlings' pandemonium in the
bushes of
            Erewhon
forget the Squares & their smorgasbord of hang-ups

But not the ordeal of the foundlings
nor the widows of Governor's Hill and Pilot's
cliff
and the stone steps to the eye of the pyramid

SIX

el la presidente

Anchors as Vaticans
for arresting an Island!
& the spots they are hooked into-
skulls, bedrooms
bank-accounts
or land lubbing

Anchoring 3 x 3
on the silt of black floors
iron flakes
but the ore of sunflares
& a smelting self
bring god-gold

Illuminating characters
shine at idyls of loving work
& heat their fates
with body light
singulars of a Black Joker
anchored in the Sun

SEVEN

the coalmine

A predisposition was set in
at the moment of first air
but the sum of the Zodiac is the goal
ah yes, for the points of power
but watch out for groggy Glutton

a half whips a half
for innermost cohesion
because the two aint meshing
women are wholes
not things nor instruments

What's behind the eyes
with a baseball bat-
somewhere there's a plenum
cut the second cord
be thine own midwife

Government's anomie
the blind eye movie
Now is all there is
& that's forever
whose

EIGHT

Cabot's Fault

The Mother eyes in defunct Americas dissolving
slowly
toward another Genesis
white West one quarter of Heaven bled

O glowing marshlands
almond chartreuse
the tides ravishing thy spongy mossbeds

sometimes the closest are the loneliest
the crack
at the lost tenderness

crows on the rim of the artesian water
a cardinal on a vein of an overdue
!

there is that sheet a life is written on
a Credo from an intimate of the Animal Kingdom
a fault fossil

a certain clocked hiatus between brothers
each in his Coffin's beach head
clasping over the Border

progenitors as forsythias
oaths as immigrating recognitions
over broken stairs

after peregrinations salvaging what
a skinful of belongings
& what inheritance

and where do Sounds go, Cabot
that a fold of time is a leap year
a greenback is a membrane

& Thou art buying and selling
the stain in the affections
the seismograph is nervous

Doctor Oblivion
psychonauts of the Od
computer equalizing

O Vulnerable, open thy Treasury
barter with it
let Chthonos legislate!

NINE

What Inn

The Light's arm
embracing distinctions

collecting them all as much
as the contemplating stones & gulls

Opal Town
bivouacked by factions

except for taverns loose
as summaries

the arc of concern
for the brooding hilled homes

light locked in its crypt of one at a time
& free as the unpredictable

the stragglers at the back door
bitten by hunches

any scrutiny's
fluid crystal light

TEN

Dogtown Songs

1

Keep your cashregister claws off
this Virgin
the skies roll over
on

2

Move over Elohim
Babson's here

3

Shades have business with cellars
the tinkle of dew
and dragon flies stitching
their wireless

4

A choice-
character or dust

5

Hunting solitaries
and lover's intercommunications
the silences have a wiccu's memoirs in them
and leaves, their punctuations

6
Hide & Seek
enjoy injoy

7
Fields running away
even as the 3 Moons of dialectics

Sable foundries
for the sanest Dogmas

8
Throw away worry
have angel hours
& lichen literatures

9
There are no classes
there is no State
for when I hear the undreamt of
it's arrived

ELEVEN

phosphorescence

I pull the plug out at 5
and all the nightbirds start whistling in my ears
trade is arrested
my hands forget the table
I'm in the bell throated song

the stars sway and the tower quivers
among them
spying out the black spaces in the music
the night is ours
and so are the throbbing arrivals and lucky squalls

the Dogbar's red flame
a bird's eye hub to the wheeling lives
the harbor is a lost
scarf of the disembarking fishermen and an old door
now as the returning sea

this Diamond less than a ball field
a telescope mound and a microscope mind
the beach sound and heather listening
around it, these and the awakened beam furtively curious
as if looking is all

TWELVE

decay

Auf Wiedersehen of childhood
Mt Adnah's judge

memory repeating
whose brush stroke, whose hand

first in front of Him
now His behind

Commerce is scouting for a Chamber
among hood rituals

better to stop a bullet
than compromise a principle

cliches are unhappy on the back of the turned cheek
a Kyrouz lens

the cult of Fakers
necklaced in skulls

the new old raping auto-suggestion
sidetracking constituents

even the pneuma's rubberoid
the 2 year Nearsighted command the august Halls

THIRTEEN

Black Sun

One's attentive
&
the unlistening

citizen hamsters
formulae go begging
dead ends diagnose

adepts geomancy quoins
& politics
for the Architecture of Love

the vasta purusha is inside Thee
electors
simmer Boss Chaos boil!

under the harbor's magnifying glass of
this Ten Pound mandala
the City's psyche is a Karnak of x-rays

all pasts are green tendrils
& so is the bone
black sun in the Sawyer Free Library

February 1975 Preface to 1976

NOTES

1. Ten Pound Light, the title, is for a lighthouse that once operated 135 years on Ten Pound Island in Gloucester Harbor.

2. "social" the colloquial for Unemployment Compensation.

3. "Kyrouz lens" is Fred J. Kyrouz, the Gloucester City Clerk, who has clear vision.

4. "Tlamatinimes" among the Inca, those who know something.

5. "vasta purusha mandala" is the Hindu symbol for Creation. It is an image of the Laws governing the Cosmos, to which men are just as subject as is the Earth on which they build. In their activity as builders, men order their environment in the same way as once in the past Brahma forced the undefined purusha (disordered existence) into a geometric form. Quoted by Mimi Lobell in her essay on "Picking Up The Pieces on Universal Order and Architecture" in ON SITE magazine, 5/6 ON ENERGY.

6. Mt Adnah Cemetery 1876 in Annisquam = Rebirth.

7. "Opal Town" opal and onyx are precious stones that have tracings of music in which there are dark interior patterns to go by. The town's real name for learning the secret truths of Nature. Stoned Light, an awareness of the divination of the Unconscious, the simultaneities of relatedness, and the alchemy of images for the transformation of self and society.

THE DREAMS / or out of the body travelling with Maximus & some others

I behold this

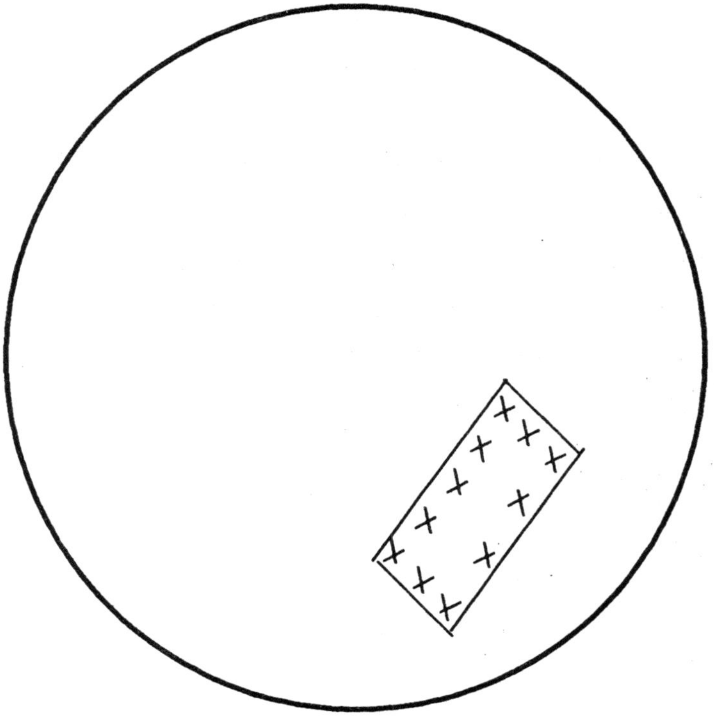

12:12 pm December 6/68   people unseal themselves

with their epithets

December 26, 1969

Charles O was reading me sections of the last part of his Epic of place, there were some humorous asides because people were giggling and savoring them, as he came to the ending I saw a special Sea: it was made of human eyes, each particular light sucked at me, I knew we had stumbled on the answers to the three Death questions, "what is it," "what is it for," and "what does it mean." Voices I had heard were breathing hard, then a cloud of contemplation fell over all of us.

THE LAST LOOK

January 1, 1970

There he was in his last room
draped in a white bedsheet
in skin & bones
the American Scald
& at his feet
his golden daughter
rubbing with camphor of the Gods
his shins, thighs, chest, shoulders
& that walnut dome
suspended in a life of its own
she, who came in as a maiden
became a woman overnight
attending to his tremors, his spleen & his Vision
shielding her sorrows
as befitting the daughter of a Poet
gentle she was with his friends
his emissaries and the mongrels after his signature
& when he wrote in a trembling hand
that never before shook
in a book most himself
for his "true believers"
my blood quaked with that scrawling
& later when the light went out
I got his message on our wavelengths
& we both know why

CAPTAIN HIKU

A string of buzzards on Ten Pound's one tooth
& Olson
at the tenement windows of his widow's walk
restless and peering

January 5, 1970

January 13, 1970

I am sitting on the couch of Dionysus
Kate is facing me
with a leather mini-miniskirt
& Charles O is scowling at her
Pull your fucking legs
together
the poet cant talk to me

You called me
Mr. God
& said
you are in danger of your life

I
was the mirror
you
spoke at

January 18, 1970

January 23, 1970

I was in an inspiring religious building, it reminded me of the original Temple of Solomon. The life mask of Olson lead me thru strangely draped rooms, where an archaic rabbi and first century scholars presided, hippies were going and coming in. The mask took me to a room where no one was around, I was down to barrels of scrolls and among them I saw a silken bound book, 5 by 5 inches, a green jade cover, and it had a title of three Jewish letters, I knew it was a new Bible of the old world for the future, and I tucked it under my coat. I was afraid I'd be caught, but the gatekeeper did not frisk me, I was protected by the mask, who said, "you will know

INTERLUDE

Two vocal beards from out of State and a silent
          one
ask me where Olson's grave is-
swinging toward the map over my monk's bed
onto the funeral carriages
and over the Bridge
to Beechbrook Cemetery
tracing the way with my pencil
I stab the gravesite
It is one of the lines
he demonstrated one night
squaring off the breath of his space-
frozen
I turn white before them
it is his lifeline on
my map
& my poem on
the Scantum and Jeffreys Basins
A Song on song

January 28, 1970

February 1st, 1970

A voice says "You killed him, He killed himself." I am looking out for him, I see him lost in the vastness of the Ocean, mists and clouds clutch at him, another party of 5 in a boat go after him. All communications are cut off. But I see him dancing on the whiteness of pages.

Dayle Stanley's dream

I am at a Wake and people are milling around, and
I went to see who was in the casket, as I neared
it and looked in, Olson woke up, climbed out, and
roared all over the funeral parlor yelling "this
is a put on to make Vincent laugh," ha ha

March 4, 1970

June 4, 1970

Charles appeared big and in perfect health
lying on the beach
he rose, approached me and we embraced.
I told him about the Reel of Allegory
and he beamed.
The angry son had come back
and was welcomed,
we walked to the water's edges,
another friend joined us
and we sang for his homecoming
and the echoes of it
rained upon the city
in a total celebration.
Then he showed us the routes to places
he thought we had never been to
but we had seen the Estate.
I had dived off a board
on Venus
and he smiled because he had known it
anyway.
We were in the world that is after this one
but it is the same
only Joy is present
in everything that lives!

September 3, 1970

Is there a life better than life, and the waves of
my hatred for this cut throat society swelled me
in its ache, and he was sitting, the American
Budda, I told Him I believed in the Second
Coming, I saw his lips move but I could not hear
him, I went closer and I read his lips and the
awful pain in his visage of a triple sadness, they
said, "do not speak to me again, go, there is only
the one first Child" I turned around and left him,
his grim voice uneasy in the pit of my being,
haunting me and him.

Charles rises, clearer than in life, out of the dense fog, solid, strong, and present in the three tenses, and he says, "THERE IS NO DEATH, we are 1000 years ahead and behind" I tell him Gerrit is having a book published by Gnosis, an important work.

I read his thoughts, "Time as we know it is not real, that I can be seen and talked with anywhere whenever and however there is a need. That the world I am in is the real world and this is what life is for, and those persons who believe it pass back and forth into either realm."

I partake of the peace of his Indwelling, I try again to engage him in a discussion of other poets, "it is not necessary that I am here to give you the message of myself as I am now."

January 10, 1971

January 27, 1971

There you were
standing inside the Fitz Hugh Lane
Stone Jug
like its ridgepole
you were talking a marathon
& I said, still going at it
when I saw your poem
on the wallboard of a classroom
& four words

like the I JING and the fourth
was "Paul"
'it is not a poem
yes it is each word
has a meaning for me
& you were not too happy
But talking was enough
& you had an EAR

March 2, 1971

Charles was in a long sleep when I went over and
viewed his features, it was round, bronzed, and in
radiant health And as I moved to touch him on his
flat iron bed with bars around him he opened his
eyes and said severely, DONT let people disturb
me, tell them they can see me only on Friday
nights and then we shook hands in the old powerful
grip of his, satisfied that we both understood
each other, he turned over and went to sleep, but
I knew he had one eye open

the house rolling with a blast of January 10, 1972

I

A Voice fron Nowhere with no body
but big as any idea
WCW hated
is saying

the grave is a JOKE
Nature is playing
with us

Time is an old coat
discarded

Okay
Free Spirit
so am I
he shouts
at me

II

Then I am at George B's house, & Charles O shows up in a long white beard down to his belt, saying our friendship's been for 57 years, over half a century

& that his daughter bought 2 paintings of Old New England that I have on my wall

I am laughing with a hand over my mouth, he's supposed to be dead & here he is twice alive

other people are picking words he dropped on the floor so busy is he designing his act on the air

he's checking out the stuff people are reading & writing with letters of the alphabet

I turn around in my sleep so I'm staring at him & wondering why did he come in to tell us what we already know

June 21, 1972

I see Persephone's river
her robes are scarlet
song is opaque
& moonlit

His erudition
my unknowing
I am in his camp now
he's in mine

I went down Fort Defiance
& saw 100 years of His shingle
the heat of his energy
still running

I see two wordless poems
a Museum
and Oxygen's
two poets

GLOUCESTER A.D. 1973

we are in an amphitheatre, this other poet who
is my shadow, and as I am his,

we are having a contest with lines that come out
of our bellies with strings of words

3500 years knocked out by Istorein

splintering the windows of one eye

the other sucked the Light in

we find out that we cannot do it alone

barber's crunch

the Lady does not think he had one

He who had balls rich as the Buddha's

at Half Moon Beach

Across all Space & Time

the Wheel is double crossed

Force at the North Station

Orpheus kneels to the Sacrifice

Maximus eats the victim

Linda Parker could become the Prioress

the First Real War since Achilles & Hector

This is the Matter

(and above us is the airplane shadow of Charles O
as a bridge of truth)

some of these words
the ghost of another poem
spoke into my left ear

Letter found among the lilies of the Night

At Fort Defiance
I saw 100 years of His shingle
the heat of his energy still running
the heart sheltering human echoes

Trespassers have a sandy plot
fake opportunity rests on
the devil's tail

How many places can you be in
o international local
It is all going furiously away
a death look on a germ of character

Persephone's river is our song's drink
her robes are scarlet, opaque and
moonlit
these words are a way of bagging the
Wind
His erudition
my unknowing
I am in his camp now
He's in mine

trailblazers hog the sidelines
perfection is their Nemesis

& the two poems
a museum
& breath's

April 1, 1973

The Zen Dream

We are at Supper, Bayliss, Anastas, Olson, myself
& some versey freaks, when Ed Kaplan expostulates
on
summarizing the prime innovators, illustrating
with
his own collage poem, one liners, zagzig, &
pictures
zeroxed from glossy ADS, when they see me as one
of
His images, they go shithouse-

Olson with his

round
Priest head oggling amazement, & in his company,
the others throwing the dirty dishes at Kaplan,
spitting
out bits of undigested food at this ballzy
teacher,
Olson disappearing into the shell of the Unicorn
he had hidden in the 28 Fort Square closet-

On the Wall of the Gloucester Daily Times I see
this
graffiti:

of all the arts,
only of the THEATRE
is everyone
an Authority
on the form,
content
and the renditions

ANON

May 1974

September 29th of the lost year

Betty & Charles come to visit me in a city of untold realities, & I tell him about a discovery I made, he looks far away, and cheated, and I say, Yes, there is nothing to talk about, you have written it all out, they quickly fade, I regret the sudden departure, Time is a rupture

I am building a precarious wall with slabs of marble, loose stones and cement, I climb to the top to survey what is on the other side but I need a string that a young woman is weaving with, she hesitates, then refuses me, she is living with her mother and is afraid of me, she likes me and I desire her, but I cannot reach her, then I know she is hiding something about herself, and I see an angel and wild beast back to back, exchanging vibrations, I go to grab the string from her, and her head snaps back into an angry cat's, I am terrified of her teeth, beholding 7 dead men in black coats and stove pipe hats in a boat coming to visit Life

Night of December 16th, 1975

I have just finished a Greek play
it is loose and mammoth
& I give it to Charles O to read
when he returns it
it is greatly chopped but a monolith
I scan the sheets
I love the towers they introduce me to
& the interlocking families
this is my real bread
I thank him
& he says it is his
I am deeply hurt and annoyed
trying to salvage what I can
I tell him
we can both sign the work
<u>No</u> he says
<u>it is mine</u>
He has swindled me
& the storm will never settle

It is morning
& I put on the crown of my watery horizon

Linda Parker's dreams told to me and as accurately as I can recapture

Vikings are at a shindig around a mead table. She and Charles approach to join them, but they are not a part of them, near the table C O presents her with a cock & an umbilical cord, the two sort of going together, as she offers him a silver goblet with wine in it

On an island are three animals, a stag, a deer, and a faun, she has been brought here in a boat with figures in it she cannot make out, she is warned that a tidal wave will come over & drown all the animals, she is fearful for them since she loves them dearly. The tidal wave arrives and drowns the deer and faun, and only the stag is left alive, somewhere, but the island is gone.

(1976)

There's a big discussion going on
Olson is sprawled on a sofa
in the middle of nowhere
& I am called to the telephone –
Nelson is on the line
& Olson cant understand why
I left him to talk with Truman,
anyway the conversation
is interrupted,
I visit him in Newburyport
Charles is pissed off
that I am leaving him behind
that I should go out of my way
to conclude a talk with Nelson
when he's in the room
waiting for me to catch his wild eyes –
But Truman's not home
he's with Charles
the silence between them
is a stone statue
one side of the face is Truman's
the other's Charles O –
& the door is closed
I cant get in
they cant get out

July 8, 1976

August 5th, another lost year

"The Big Oral Kid" Socrates, he has no use for him.
Ah, himself.

Charles dived, the bulk of him fell flat on the granulated thick water, and he swam with his face down, I worried about it, how did he manage it without breathing, as he went out to Sea. Then he is naked, and old, the patriarch, surrounded by a clutch of kids, several of them kissing his prick, he lying down like a Potentate, but his life seems finished. He is showing stacks of Mss and portfolios of paintings, no one knew he had done them, I am astounded at the amount of this unexpected production, that no one had even dreamt about, the places moved me, I could not believe it, I had been let into his closet.

Dayle Stanley, "The Social Dike", a miscalculation of his perceptions.

I am clutching her body length and she is stuck fast to me as I am to her, I had never experienced such a stuck condition before, I could not let go, neither could she, we so much wanted to be joined together as one 2 bodied person. Then she has her back to me and we are embracing each other as each is absorbed by the other.

He is showing me a portion of a long poem he is working on, and I let him peruse a page of a big poem I am at. He is pleased, and invites me to a reading he is going to. We have front row seats.

3 persons come on the stage, then a fourth, an Englishman, about 40, begins reading in Indian from the Mahabharata, I cannot follow him but I am enchanted, suddenly Indians in long robes in one color of the rainbow, each different, gather around him. And I wonder is this the way they do it in India. I feel left out, the Mahabharata is the rim of the circle. I turn to Charles, the seat is empty.

August 7, 1976

Charles O is convalescing and surrounded with a lot of old people and students, but he is really dying and is angry that some persons think so, he is that fucked Mountain, and I am attending to him, wanting him to kick the bucket, he is lecturing and yakking from a bedchair, in his white toga, and I am impatient with his sense of continuance, he is pissed off at me for the same thought, anyway he desires to take up somewhere special, and I can't figure why he's so active, and plunging ahead, he is in my car, and we are nearing my new altar, he backs the car into my driveway and succeeds looking forward, as he turns and winks at me.

November 3/1977

Night of the 2 Dead Men

I meet Charles somewhere in a Cameo, and he is wearing that hat in the Photo at O'Neill's bookshop in Cambridge, he is regal and stately

and I glance back on the whole experience and enjoy every morsel left I am on the outside, and the future unfolding is almost as I planned it, and he says, Remember I told you your time will come and we will look back and forward together, only I am ahead of you, but not really since you are in my dream as I am in yours.

Then I see my father, reading a manuscript of mine, and he is trying to grasp the contents, he raises his head, and queries me about sections and phrases, and is pleased, "You have ten poems that will last" as he turns pale, sad, and sorry he has not been more open to my madness.

The real reel of August 7th, 1978

Ralph Luce told me he saw my words in Olson's
poem, <u>no death</u> -
I went to recheck my Long Song
which was sleeping in the back burner.
My copy was in the house on the Fair View
grounds, but the last words were
"rites of a working man"
Peg & the kids were shadow people
in the kitchen -
Olson's figure was a fog
over the Fair View
when the bell rang at 5:31
to awaken me for the ceremony
on Bass Rocks
as a symbolic demonstration
to remember the A bombing of
Hiroshima
33 years ago
as Richard drenched 2 manikins
A Mother & Child with kerosene
I rang the bell 31 times
& Barbara twice
I got terribly nauseated

seeing the flaming manikins
I asked Richard to take
the burnt Mother & Child
to the Hospital
& he said "They'll think
we are really crazy-"
like fantasy & reality
the 2 no deaths

the Dark May 5th, 1980

I am at George Butterick's house, and Charles
O shows up in a slept in ragged beard
saying our friendship's been for 57 years,
over half a century, that his daughter
bought 2 paintings of Old England that's
on my wall in Gloucester, I am laughing
with my hand over my mouth thinking he's
still yakking to beat the town, other people
are straggling in to catch his lecture,
he's checking out the stuff I am working
on, and I am thinking he's preparing to
whack me, but he can't see me, so absorbed
is he in gesturing information out, I turn
in my sleep so I'm staring up at him
wondering, did he come for Eva Matz's
benefit, she who is stealing the show
with her abstract mural rug as I am writing
Adolph's name on a cave wall underground
the Pyrenees, as Eva's new rug discovers
The Beginning at Coitus Avenue, Charles
is annoyed as hell for her distracting me,
and he goes off with George to some
Castle cellar, his arm around George's
shoulder, Peter Anastas and his Dogtown
people are working with clay for some
sculpture words are going to design

to save Babson's reservoir from the
waterkillers, on the boulders are Olson's
Maxims, in letters bigger than Babson's

I HAD TO LEARN THE SIMPLEST THINGS LAST

The 4th of July, 1981

He did not want to come back
& here he was surrounded with all his
acolytes & hangers on
all the afficionados & he did not
want to talk
but his friends were glad he was
back for good
until he started to tell them
his whole doctrine
was passe, that he was not a
manufacturer, that he was not a
a factory for mental gymnastics
or parts for a retail business-
They were aghast & disappointed
how could he return
& tell this
he said he had done what he
had to do & now it was all of no use
to him

He stared at them with his saucer eyes
        & said find your own cups
dont follow my dead life
        because he is in his real life
& desires no connection with theirs
        again they were astounded
"Find your heaven
        I'm in mine"
I sized him up, they felt
        abandoned
was it for this they had pledged
        their lives & fortunes
that their real life was with
        him
now in the other world
        & theirs is only the shadow
of His
        They seemed to understand
but it was too late but if they
        could drop him & make it
in the shadow world they'd
        have it, the only glimmer

of hope as he vanished
he had stained their souls
in the world of literature
& were not in this life
they were in death
he is in life
They are in the Past
He's in the Future
& I'm the 2 arms of them
I tried to convince them
but their ears were clogged with
hard overflowing wax

STRANGE TRINITY

Cid is showing Charles & me his new poem
on large sheets of Japanese paper
each poem about five or twelve words
floating on a background
of subdued mauve, green, amber
& starry blues
presenting them as a Tarot deck
He's on top of the Mountain
& on his way down
as Charles uses little oblong
black stickers for blotting out
un-necessary words & disclosures
Still on the peak, Cid is,
a kind of word samurai
preparing to descend
to the valley river
Charles is mulling over
this American Jap flying on his
Paper Moon
taken by the orientals
when he's as good as they are
but he's not in his Dorchester village
he's wanting the Buddha
of poetry
to approve his sword game
who is saying

stay with the masses
we've had enough of Lordship
& high tide
is calling us
as Charles turns to me
"he hasnt heard
a fucking word
he thinks he's pure
art
he'll never make it across
the Pacific again"
I spy the scimitar
in Charles' right eye
& Cid descending Mt Fuji
in his left,
& we are three brothers
come together for a reconnoitering
people's footprints are everywhere
& I hear
HEY, POET!
We have ears!
but Charles O & Cid
are bathing their feet
in the river water
talking about old times

January 12, 1982

the coat **january 19, 1982**

At Helen Stein's ferry a man is regaling a group
about the time he heard Olson offering me his
overcoat as a gift after he dies
                                                        but Elaine
Wing was not listening & it irritated me
that she intentionally ignored the main tale as
well as the affinities Peter Anastas said is the
mortar
                    anyway he was gesticulating how
Olson & Ferrini were having an argument about the
promise he was making, that I couldnt seem to
accept such a present as it was too large
but Olson kept shrugging it off Oh it could be tailored
to accomodate my figure, but I dont have that
kind of money
                    I tried to remember how he rumpled
his hearers & joked about the schism when there
wasnt any to begin with
                                                        I wondered again why
Elaine wasnt interested, yet Helen made the
Amerindian sign that said the Great Spirit is
the Adam & Eve I AM
                                                        furthermore Kathleen's
old all purpose coat fit me better

I couldnt locate the 3
pennies as I prowled at
every corner in the house
I poked into all the pockets
of the secondhand clothes
outside in the yard
I uncovered one bright penny
under wet catshit
a dime under the gas-stove
& an Eire shilling with
Cuchulain & Pearse
in a Minoan clay pot-
I tossed them up
& they gave me
THE BOOK OF ISIS
it was from Charles' battered
typewriter-
The new pyramid
with Her eye ruling-
She's in my sarcophagus
with me
I'm her then
she's my now
our one
Child
we are

January 30th, 1982 intersection

poesia & the literary techniks of it
as a scribe said
"look at the mythologies of the Sidhe & you
find my hand with his, yet neither is ours
one will slaughter you for the pigs
another will see your crystal ball
as MAEVE does who first gave it to you
glistening with lovelight"

I caught him among the book stacks
in the cellar of Goblin Library
stealing images
& he was eating Yeats' arm,
I saw a Deacon sucking on the fingernails
a dwarf in the big man's belly

the two of them
in my Folk cave

my brother was telling me
as I was combing Half Moon Beach
look
dream's language
is undulating inside a couple dancing on springwater
& no words

the rooms were thick with a moth dust
clouds of them under the furniture
in the corners sitting on chairs
I didn't know if I'd ever get the sunlight in again
but I was rich with the poem
I kept repeating in my mind
so's I wouldnt forget it
when I woke up
but it went on another trip

as Hermes Trismegistus came in

The Spinning Wheel of November 10, 1983

it was a meeting of the four corners
the lady of the round features accepted
my Moon-man & became deliciously free
the earlier woman left the open hospital
with the diagram of her soul
Vishnu destroyed the continents & islands
I recognized mortality
as I licked Vishnu
with a New Earth

A pin point of starlight
came at me
from behind the sightseen galaxies
looming at me
with the scrubby beard of Charles O
smiling approval
when I said
few people have the sense of history
or the evolution of consciousness
for satisfying
our daily living

THE PUBLIC LOVE LETTERS

Dear Citizens:

Roy W. Griffin's double-barrelled letter in the Times March 30th had a conciseness of thinking and writing that lifted me off my chair.

I regret not being present at that Council meeting, and like thousands absent, what I want to know is:

was Griffin correct or was he not, when he spoke and wrote about Fees and Rights dealing with public property?

Since the City Council has a habit of being in-effectual and making mistakes, was it wrong in confiscating the clam beds?

March 31/1979

The "first" big nuclear leak at Three Mile Island, and I am nervous about Seabrook NH over our heads, remembering the sizzling Japanese of Hiroshima and Nagasaki, and worrying about the citizens of Harrisburg and environs, wanting to bestow on inter-relatedness and interdependence Parenthood, concluding that only Catastrophe is the Example that teaches sometimes, and here I am in my own way forestalling the Great Disaster in spite of the inevitable Fact that people are expendable, so live today, get all you can and frig tomorrow, terredo the children unborn and those already conditioned by a dis-eased society, that the State triumphs, Leakage or no, that the end is coming what can you do about it, but boyoboy what these accidents, and there are none as such, are showing us as the nightmare routine dulls us, as the clear mind bursting upon ah the Un-utilized, the miraculous opposite, at our behest, still facing this Present we are the makers of and the victims and witnessing our forefathers admonishing us with "why cant you connect with the revolutionary instructions we have given you, so sit if you can, on your nuclear nests !"

April 2/1979

Ugliness, any form of it, is our commercial heritage. Esthetics is good business, some have discovered. We have a few architects who might know how to relate the sky-scenes to the wharf-embraces to the harbor-lines to the sea's place. Let us erect around these unities a complex we can be proud of by keeping a vigilant eye on Ecosystems, and we will be doing Justice to our community, our economy, and our children, IN SPITE of a plutonium Seabrook on top of our heads, the ever-persisting reminder of the Ugliest of all.

April 6th/1979

Sanctuary a key to wholesomeness

Enter the re-inforcements of oil: the Chamber of Commerce.

Because opposing values divide us, because the enemy is always within, because survival is the goad to the goal, because success is measured by the money games which created the atomic mushrooms and the oil spills, because to co-operate like the Food Co-op is the way of the future, so is the marine sanctuary the first step toward a wholesome earth.

Therefore I suggest that we ask the children to help us dialogue and legislate, and utilizing them, do better than our parents did before us.

The fishes and the birds are calling for the children.

Oct. 15/1979

Carter not listening to the music

Obscene, the way Carter is manipulating the American malaise by his promise to protect the Persian Gulf oil routes with the blood of a new generation, just to win a second term in the White House. The young did not ask to be born, nor to be thrown to the wolves of war before they've even begun to live.

The polls of the fickle are supporting the media and filling Jimmy's tank. The evil behind any flag. Be a patriot for oil.

Remember the old song, you can fool some of the people some of the time, but not all the people all the time - well, Carter's banking on obsolete chauvinism to keep him King of the Hill, and he's hardly out of swaddling clothes, a super, Bible-back, Christian stuck in the blunders of foreign policies based on three-legged fear now turned gun-metal.

This undersized, oversized peace-maker subverting the problems at home with threats of war, a man with a mission of global misery, secretly gloating over his ascending popularity by his lucky diplomacies.

World War II took us out of the collapse of the markets of the 30s,and according to the Carter

Doctrine of enclosure, World War II is the skyway to universal prosperity.

Perhaps Jimmy Carter is the last of the mini-megalomaniacs. Ah, to see the old dodders who make wars forced to fight them with their over-the-hill figures.

O Aristophanes, where are you?

Now the draft. During the other Great Depression, it was the WPA, the PWA, the CCC, that saved the system. Now the draft is to give Carter a boost to his flagging campaign. So let the recruits march to the towns and cities and help clean and straighten them out. Start with the potholes, then go after the garbage the health departments cannot cope with, then the neighborhoods that are slumped in decaying losses, and this will be creative target practicing. Let the draft match the WPA as records for the books to come.

One thing is certain, and that is that other nations are moving fast establishing their Declarations of Independence, a document we may have to reapply,(with 393 years under our craniums) try the next phase it suggests, designing a world Charter of Economic Interdependences for seeding a United States of Love. If you think this is too far out, ask the planetary kids.

For throughout the land, outcroppings of intelligences are acting as instrumentalities of holistic correspondences.

If we can visualize the future, the past will be ahead of us.

Carter's not listening to this underground music, he's in the grip of the Mirror, he's offbeat, brooding about his statesmanship in the history journals, a puppet in the back pocket of the arch-strategist of crumbling empires, Dr. Kissinger.

February 20/1980

I have heard all the arguments and listened to the passion of Joe Orange for the preservation of our living water.

A loss of 9,000,000 gallons is a hell of a lot of water in a drought, and most of us can remember and still see that iron pipe laid out on the side of the road going from here to Ipswich in an attempt to save Gloucester.

Why, why cant the EDIC and the Plannners move that road off the edge of the watershed?

Dont let this new encroachment on the great gift of Babson to Gloucester's life become the dead Tom Welch in our dory on a shrinking watershed.

April 4/80

Uniting opposites

Once we understand the disease of schizophrenia we shall be on the track of some answers to the problems we are all faced with.

Simply put: I feel the 80s will be engaged primarily with healing the split between man and woman, spirit and body, church and state, profit and labor, war and peace, and all the so called irreconcilable opposites.

The Moonies are just an example of some people, like the second born Christians, trying to come to grips with the conditioning process.

The Moonies have found themselves, due to their naivete or wisdom, sitting on the tiger's tongue, can they pull off the conditioning process.

This is the meaning and demonstration of uniting the opposites: die to the old ways, open the eye of the belly button, listen to the new song of the unity sleeping inside you.

How much more of our pollution is Mother Earth going to take, dont think Mt. St. Helens is only a volcano.

July 3/1980

Can Gloucester doctor itself?

The time has come for Gloucester to deliberate its limits of growth. To stabilize it, monitor its population, hold to its open vistas, its sense of smallness the laurels of its individual flavors, that the goals are not for material wealth. Can we begin the difficult task of evaluating our values: dare we take this initiative? Or continue as usual being the victims of monied circumstances because we lack the fortitude of dealing with the nitty-gritty, the basic building blocks of living through loving.

Is fishing the heart valve of this town, can the fresh fish flee, thrive over the foreign vessels with their vaults of frozen fish and the everpresent threat of oil spills?

Can Gloucester bring together the Word and the Deed for their unexpected dancing forms?

Or is our Fate beyond our control?

Are our descendants to repeat our hangups differently?

Or has the die been cut, is Spengler right with his DECLINE OF AMERICA, can any town set an example, or have we gone as far out and as far in as we have, can these mental extremities be brought together, like what's between the North and the South Poles?

Why were some souls ripe for following headlong into Reverend Jones's death creed, and how many more bewitched by Hog Moon, the self promoting messiah of himself, the Big Nuts sporting solid gold Cadillacs, and the little bolts locked in bedlam?

Simply put: Can Gloucester be doctor to itself, and measure its debts and credits, balance the sheets off on you get what you give, that self, family and community are one, and their division is the brainwork of the ills any society is heir to.

Dare we design and work toward unselfish interests for the limits of growth and profit sharing, and show the rest of the nation that as a city we are hewing out a social consciousness through the democratic exchanges setting the island on its feet and in its gut, instead of on its head, subjected to the tidal waves of personal neurosis and economic inequalities?

I throw this upon all citizens as a starter, or shall we meet matters haphazardly, and leave the results to plague the oncoming generations, for them to correct because we were afraid to?

Is the dictum: Don't tamper with see-saw?

July 17/1980

The harbor is our house

The harbor is our kitchen, bedroom, playroom, work-area, and cellar. As our homes are so is the harbor. Many hundreds earn their livelihood immersed in the stink, and do not complain, it is their bread and bill-payer. Since they do not share in the profits, then the fish companies should pour some of that wealth into cleaning up their daily acts. The vessels might have reverence for the seas which give them the bounties of their trips.

If some emancipated captains succeed in developing, with the generosity of the city, a Fishermen's Co-Operative, then let us learn from that lesson.

Only mutual interest in the harbor and the Annisquam Strait is the real road to a solution.

The earlier settlers did not reckon with their future, our present, so their short vision is our mess.

Therefore: Leo can extend the bubbler further out, he can stop the fish companies pouring their refuse into the basin, and with the help of the Board of Health correct the sewer problem. He can triumph with Carolyn O'Connor, Edward

MacLeod, Frank Rose, and Jim Munn. Then tackle the Annisquam crap with the good faith of the homeowners. With a will, directions follow.

With this year and a half left, Alper's administration can become Gloucester's finest monument.

The people are hot on the track now. We cannot fail.

We can say we did it together: After the years of the Great Stink, we knocked off that infamous adage tied to Gloucester's tail.

And continuing with this dedicated teamwork steal the Moonies' thunder!

August 20/1980

" We are a see-town ! "

Some day, one day, which is present, the star system will be recognized for being closer than just there in the skies.

When some little or unknown people from Newburyport, our sister sea town, put on Jacques Brel is Alive and Living in Gloucester at the Blackburn Tavern, only a few of the actors were professional, most of them lifted that play to standing ovations, Theresa was so genuine she drew tears from my looking and hearing, and she was one of eight, and three musicians, who electrified Fishtown.

That day, which is here, is full of living theatre, there are persons here at the edge of raising life to an art, who dont need to watch others act for them. There are restless poems, nodding plays, fluid paintings, talking stories, moving sculptures, and whatnot, who dont need to be exploited for the strictures of self-aggrandizement. Once in the ground of optimum creation, and we function at a minimum, everyone will be thriving at their fructifying potential, each and everyone in the community participating in whatever form erupts into action.

A miraculous example is the poetry of mental patients at NorHaven, Minn. Each of the isolated ones are living out their poems, and a number of them writing them down on paper with aid of an assistant who understands. Each patient is included. Each accepted on her terms, these people happen to be women, and they published a book, "Thief of Sadness," the title of one of the poems, the drawings are like children's, and so are the faces of the group on the back cover, therein expanding indentities.

The Newburyport actors did it for Jacques Brel, their next play could be on our sea town, the mentally retarded at NorHaven did it for the poems in themselves, and they are working on their keepers.

There are persons in town ready to do it for a theatre of all the arts, the famous are here in this holy local, totally loco with the joys and tragedies.

I am posting the idea that the human stars on earth do match all those above, for no human is excluded, as no starlight is, then it wont be the things to <u>own</u> that enrich life. We start by giving ourselves away like children do their pictures, poems, songs, or stories, because there is more where they come from, thereby riding the Winds of Time.

Because there is no separation, everything is connected, for everything that lives is immortal, and we know it, and as we act on it, so will the flowers know, the trees, the marshlands, Dogtown, oxygen, the drinking water, and so will the differences that divide us, for the magical is in the fully living, working, playing at the transforming potential, only the local can awaken, this community is inside one, is the personal discovery, and the insider, phosphorescing all the senses of a new awareness.

As a Zen master said, "If you see, see immediately, don't wobble" and we are a see-town!

September11/1980

Let's not kowtow

The issue of the water supply is not yet settled despite the majority vote of the City Council, not by a ram shot.

If Peg Sibley stopped the machinery of its destruction and failed that night of Sept. 16th, the water itself has something to say, inevitably.

If Carolyn O'Connor raised objections on the layout of the watershed, and they are legitimate, then blessed be her continued gumption for finding our positions on this map, and where are the others?

If Marion Rogers dug up the facts to forestall the possible pollution of Babson's Reservoir, her work is a warning we had all better heed.

If Joe Orange, who knows every inch of the roads around the watershed, can not sleep nights, he has damn good images as the little litter cleaners found.

If John Sutherland is persistent, it is because certain details and unanswered questions bug him and us, and that at the heart of this over-riding business, the real pulse, the interrelationships between land and water, is missing.

If Fred Brown is impatient and irritated with the delay perhaps that last City Hall meeting will impress him with the anxiety people feel about leaving no stone unturned, and he might learn that humble patience is becoming for a public servant.

No one is against jobs and new industry, the concern is that whatever we undertake we do it right, no mistakes allowed, not one fraction of an error when the watershed can be undermined, and our lifeblood poisoned.

An offering full of unforeseen consequences.

Can't you see that? Are the proponents so intransigent that they will reckon with a chaos unlimited?

Well, there are citizens who do not want to gamble on that chance, and that is why Peg Sibley and Carolyn O'Connor tried to gain more time, even though edict has done all that it can, it still has not appeased our fears, because we are still worried and vigilant.

Do you think the majority is always right? Even The Gloucester Daily Times is tired of the process, and has opted for the disaster, unbelievable.

With the land available, we say change your plans, try for that alternative route, it is not a matter of do it right now or die, with Gus Foote suffering in the middle of that quandary, let this be one of the peaks in our history when we did not kowtow for another and deadlier, snafu.

September 19/1980

I was ashamed for our city

During all my years participating in and studying the democratic gladiator games, I have seldom witnessed a City Council put an iron muzzle upon a woman's tongue.

I was ashamed for our city, disgusted, and appalled.

Was it because there were merely two handfuls of voters in that audience, and thus they felt they could get away with that ingrate action, ungentle and so cowardly, the polite stench of a civilized deus ex machina.

Six members, spearheaded by McCormack, used their streamroller over a representative of the Fishermen's Wives, Peg Sibley, subverting her challenge to revive a lost case.

All because Carey, a man with some courtesy, made a motion to allow her, a constituent of his ward, to let off steam.

Was it because they are tired of her adamant position, her fire, her emotional eloquence, her fierce determination to carry the battle over the bitter end, and was it because she made them appear as parliamentarian robots in the service of an approved Error which Time may throw up, let us pray not.

No wonder people avoid the weak theater of many Council meetings, unless personally involved, well that night was a classic show box.

And rearing again in a sneak view the ugly masks of some sexist attitudes, a lot of intelligent women stay away from that arena because they know they dont stand a snowstorm's dance in Hades.

Democracy could really jive with more women uniting their private lives to public law-making, for they are the lighthouses of the new consciousness.

The fisherwoman!

That six gun butt Peg Sibley's lips just long enough for her to catch back her mind's breath.

So they let her speak for a few moments before the bell rang.

Ah, yes, that grave night they turned the last screw in the coffin of their decision EDIC will sport as a neck-piece.

October 13/1980

Dear Council Members:

DOGTOWN is Gloucester's sacred territory.

Keep those buzzing monsters of the devil off our holy land!

Once they go up, we'll have them sawing in our sleep, sawing the ghosts of the first settlers, sawing second thoughts too late, sawing bird watchers, sawing moonshine hunters, sawing dedicated runners, sawing sightseers, sawing blizzards, sawing pollen, sawing wild birds, and sawing the last vestige of Peace in the heart of this island.

How dare they disturb this salt-air wilderness.

Just dont let these Wind Power entrepreneurs strap their row of metallic aliens to our beloved sanctuary!

October 27/1980

GEORGES should be off limits

The Oil Monopolies must leave Georges Bank alone.

There are no safeguards.

Can you see those matchstick rigs in the maw of storms, blizzards, hurricanes?

Can you see the black vomit?

There is only one perfect solution, and that is what people of clear vision in Gloucester, New Bedford, and other fishing villages know and still fight for:

Make Georges Bank a Marine Sanctuary, nothing less!

AND if the Government wont understand how simple and concise this problem is, then I suggest that we the courageous, the working people, the fishermen, and the fisherwomen of the New England coast take matters into our own hands, and trusting the Bible of the Declaration of Independence, overturn Government decision.

Yes, this is revolution, and we have been given instructions, for every form of negotiation so far, as we have seen and heard, is daily and nightly courting the Death of Georges Bank.

So, tune in your ingenuities!

Nov 20/1980

Do you know what time it is

I beg to take issue with your editorial of December 29th, that the USA train runs better between the extremes: because my reading of society tells me that the live track is the third rail whatever it may be, that the useful information comes through the third ear and the third eye.

Thesis, antithesis, and synthesis, for if you remember a Brain said that if you dont learn from History you are condemned to repeat it.

The Colonies revolted against the Right Royalists abroad and at home: the North fought against the Right South and their Slavery: today ERA against the stuck roles of womankind.

What do you think is going on in South and Central Americas, twiddledewinks, their birthpangs are terrible to witness, look at all the stillborns, the horrible miscarriages.

To take the position against the Status Quo is to confront the realities that mis-shape all avenues of life.

To shy away from that third rail is to be Dodo.

Going back via Reagan to what basics, easier bucks for Corporate Capital and corporate individual? So, give Big Business a crack at

Incentive, (there are healthier incentives but they will choose the sick incentives) which will solve Inflation, my my, so bring back the good ole days and years, pity poor Capital, it will straighten the cooked and crooked legs of the Economy.

How safe can you play it?

Do you know what time it is?

Let me tell you about some of its faces.

There is an Earth Time, which is running hell-bent against itself, because Exploitation is the first Priority, conservation second, and we know who reap the benefits. There is enough lethal weaponry to blast the Earth out of the Solar Combine, or make it a brown Moon. Yet even if that should happen, an invincible Spirit will burst it into bloom again!

There is Technological Time, which means Invention is undermining the whole concept of Labor and Capital, the robots and the computers are already here, and the people are baffled.

There is Leisure Time, is humanity ready for that?

There is Cosmic Time, a major earthquake is predicted by some scientists for August 10th off the shores of Peru that will awash New Zealand and Australia, and the West Coast of both Americas, that's for 1981, 1982 all the planets line up as an electrical arrow in the Heavens.

There is Psycho-social Time, Animal Time, Atom Time, Spontaneous Time, and opposite to Death Time there is Musical Instrument Time, and Joy in the dances of Soul Time, a kin to Love Time, the best of all.

Simply put, not to risk anything is to do nothing, vegetate, let Inflation go haywire, let Crime go hogwild, forget the money is our Creed!

What we are faced with is a complete overhaul of our present attitudes by coming to grips with every crucial issue, and giving birth to another way of behaving, we have to dare it, where is that Pioneer exuberance, when it is needed most? Safe with the three monkeys?

Now do you see what I mean, it <u>is</u> possible to bring about easy birth, but the forces of our destinies, and I pinpoint specifically, the two Ruling Parties just wont allow the changes crying to exercise the real play of working to save our rudderless Republic, and the suffering Earth.

Do you realize that some 48% of the voters refused to go to the polls, you can almost say that the elected Party in office is illegal!

Stay still in the trough of dont stick your neck out and you lose by default. You are not in the game. You have brainwashed yourself out of the picture.

Read between the lines and listen with that third ear, a magical Co-operation is active in unobtrusive endeavors, but those in Power places know in their cells that their security rests on deep mud.

January 1st/1981

It took the son of a military man to explain anarchy in a letter to the Gloucester Daily Times of 7/21/79 when he succinctly stated:

> A system certainly cannot cope
> when it is based on imposed
> authority, on law and order.
> Anarchy rejects authority and
> emphasizes personal responsibility,
> consciousness, and consequence.
> Rather than control, self control;
> rather than order, self order;
> rather than law, love.
> How can a civilization develop
> these values? Not by rules
> (the substitution of formulae
> for thought) nor punishment
> (fear for self examination).
> Not by a God of wrath and
> commandments.

Vandalism occurs in the absence of
responsibility, consciousness
and consequence: in the filling
of marshlands, the construction
of nuclear plants, the forcing
of children into molds for
parental convenience, the proffering
of safety, security, and salvation
in package deals.
Anarchy turns on creation rather
than reaction.

Martin Ray's letter is on the waters of my Map of Gloucester. Saved from oblivion.

My neighbor down the street.

January 1st/1981

O brave Conservation Commission

Imagine the stupidity and the gall of the EDICT hellbent for running a road across the watershed and diverting a natural spring for industrial expansion. It crinkles the mind, and tramples the emotions, that arrogance in the face of our current and persistent water shortages.

Do we need a skyscraper village on our island reservation?

A suave claque of one dimensional mentality tampering with Gloucester's aqua vitae, in the name of acquiring jobs. Common sense is given a kick in the groin by these despoilers of wetlands, and they almost got away with it had it not been for that-never-give-up John Sutherland and two holistic hounds from that town next door, Tim Costello and Larry Stepenuch, plus a few veterans of vigilance.

Yeah. "That's Democracy" doctor Brown, what do you crave, autocracy?

O, brave Conservation Commission, we pay homage to your courage, clarity, far-sightedness, and strength of conviction!

The City of Gloucester via the City Council gave EDICT the land for industrial development. The city is notorious for monumental boners. Perhaps an aroused citizenry of new and old blood can reverse that order and take away from EDICT the 70 acres left for that enterprise. There is plenty of room elsewhere, there are enough buildings and businesses at Blackburn Park.

Let us not undo Howard Blackburn's acts of heroism with developers' bug eyed visions!

The watershed is drying and crying out loud: give us all the elbow spaces we had in the first place, don't choke our vital substances for you whom we nourish.

Do you think after you've killed us that you will be able to build a lake in the sky for drinking and purifying yourselves?

We warn you, you are endangering the physical balance of Dogtown by persisting in a disaster coaster. Our sacred axis has no earth-mind for if you don't believe us, walk our whole area, swathe your eyes around and inside yourselves, put your ears to the ground, you will hear a battle going on between discordances and celestial harmonies, underworld and over, for as people of a place are, so is the land and the sea.

Tuesday, January 27/1981

All from a single seed

On the nature of the Center and the Circumference:

A. The Top of the Harbor as Bastille #1.
Knowlton's Field in Toytown, Bastille #2.
Iron Village (EDICT) on Dogtown's drinking water, #3.
Hawthorne Bastille in Ward One, #4,

ah poor knighted Michael Harrington,
the wonder congressman, turned
pewter.

The 2 deep freeze penitentiaries on the inner Harbor.

Washington DC is the Hub, American the Rim of the Wheel, and Gloucester, a spoke.

Is the picture clear, can you see Time and Space in Action?

B. Haig and Reagan shoving us, at a misread mandate from the masses, into 4 years of Purgatory.

Remember the prediction for 1984, by Orwell?

Are we self-prophesing it with the last gasp of Predatory Enterprise?

The Country built on Revolution afraid of its roots?

Hang around, the wheel is rolling faster into the reeks of Hell, 2 1/2 with its attendant horrors the loss of jobs and schools, families being stepped on by the steel heel, and the extremities of the survivors.

America helped strangle Chile, O keep out of San Salvador, the blood of Vietnam is still on our conscience.

There are people with eyes wide open, who understand more than they speak about, who will stop with the Power of our Song the Neutron Bomb in midair!

C. With this hub as an eye we are never helpless, in spite of the "I am only one what can I do" it all springs from a single seed!

March 13/1981

Raping the commission

So with a few mosquito-eyed members and one dive bomber with the heavy voice, the Jobs man of the big foot on the City Council are bent on raping the Conservation Commission.

They must think the citizens crawl on all fours, these killers of the Beautiful, with their "but you cant eat it", yeah, we have human eyes and do!

April 8/1981

Conservationists supported

Dear City Council, please listen, dont tamper with or gut the Conservation Commission.

They are the custodians to the liberties of the beautiful.

The necessities are grounded here and so are the jobs and relationships.

Husband this real wealth.

Our human springs are here in the spirit's optimum, not the minimum we have been so used to, and so many have settled for.

It is the less that continually depletes our vitalities, when our divine energies are aching to re-create.

Beware of mosquito visions.

The Conservation Commission is the primary mind of our city government, do not strip it, give it more strength.

April 10/1981

May they listen to their consciences

I am praying that the Conservation Commission will not buckle under the railroading tactic by EDICT and the Planning Board to break their back, as was obvious from a joint meeting of three ruling bodies of city government.

Mr. Schernig is the hammer man, and he is clearly pounding the stake into Babson's living body, in spite of the Ad Hoc Committee's convincing propoal for a better road.

After the Conservation Commission passed on Keep Off Babson's Watershed, EDICT returned, rearmed with a slight modification with their original route, and loosened their hounds, the Planning Board for the feast.

These bulldogs of economic progress are in cahoots to industrialize the Heartland of Gloucester, imagine, if you can, the short and long consequences ...

The last defenders of our environment, and the quality of beauty most of us live here for, is the Conservation Commission, may they stand loyal to the principles they are a committee by, may they listen to their conscience, alone as so often happens, against the onslaughts of Decay, as we concerned citizens rally behind them.

June 12, 1981

Gamble not with watershed

I was one of the public not invited to speak, in fact I was shut off by A. Andrade, Chairman of that meeting, when I tried to ask a simple question.

It was a whackshop of the three committees, the Planning Board, EDICT, and the Conservation Commission, an ingroup activity and the public excluded, OK, lesson learned.

The attempt of the Planning Board & EDICT is still to run a road over the WATERSHED, even though they paid lip service to being open minded in looking for another way out of our dilemna, but they are as tight minded as some of us about the preservation of the watershed for this generation and the others coming.

As Bill Cahill reported in a lead article on the Gloucester Daily Times, BABSON WATER-SHED TOO GOOD TO LOSE, April 11, 1981, and capped the argument for saving our life feeder with a quote by Dick Souza when he said "Protection and expansion of the city's water supply rates top priority over industrial expansion, dont get me wrong, I'm all for industrial expansion, and more jobs, but we need water first."

Since the memory of the public has to be refreshened with rainfall, I suggest that the Times do what they rarely if ever do, and that is reprint Cahill's essay, which is clear, concise, geograph-ical, historical, environmental, a perfect picture of the terrain in question, especially when the whole issue has come to the Crossroad: Jeopardize the Watershed, Or locate another area for Industrial Growth.

Toneatti was adamant and insightful, as one keen member of the Planning Board, who picked up on Toneatti's simple articulate understanding of the problem. Supporting these two we say: look elsewhere, there are enough industries on that Hill. Varian-Extrion Corp and the Medical Center are on watershed land.

Stop monkeying around with what cannot be replaced!

My question is: If Dr. Schernig and EDICT have the economic future and the welfare of Gloucester as their goal, why will they risk the destruction of what we as a city cannot live without?

NO TRESPASSING HERE.

Gamble as is your hearts' desires, and your pocketbooks' but never with the Watershed.

THAT you have no right to do.

June 29/1981

If the councilors and the audience, during the Hawthorne labor pain, did not hear the frustrations of an elder dame of solid green cloth, a mistress of music and an iconoclast, who demanded that the said councilors, and one end man in particular, lift their voices so that they could deliver their views openly, if they mis-read the boiling steam of this Lady, then they are all historic witnesses, or merely insensitive office-holders, very dense indeed, because her unsettling behavior and 2 slamming exits indicated louder than talk, her angry disgust with the martinet procedures of the said magistrates, and one loyally battered dissenter, of an unbalanced future

these selected surgeons of protocol used very deft and skillful scalpels to hew and reconstruct the Hawthorne Condos to specifications hoping to satisfy everyone, some private investors, and incensing a few disgruntled individuals fighting the steamroller, these lawmakers laying on the outer shores of the harbor, blotting out wild spaces, a piece of collective architecture only the very rich can occupy, which is what the land is free for, if you cannot make a million bucks it's your own fault, money buys everything and anything, and we learn this with our grade school milk,

may Time reveal that mystery woman
who captured that council meeting on a canvas of
memory saying if you dont catch the Devil at his
workshop dont cry after he has stolen the safe

July 8/1981

The spiritual protein of my diet is the Bostonia Globe, and our homehigh amphitheatre, both keeping me in shape for penetrating appearances.

Since a dialogue is crucial between the written media & the readers, an active confrontation is constantly effected, railed at some times, other times silently swallowed, or shouted at, or dealt with by letters, any policy restricting the variety of expression is a loss for any old new game in this playground of democracy.

Since the daily newsprint is closest to my art, which works best through immediate sharing, I feel myself as a running undercurrent in the tides of spontaneous information and the interweaving rhythms, therefore being thus involved with all that's rapidly happening on so many fronts, one of the whirlpools sucks me in, & I rise with Song, like the approaching

BALLAD OF THE MOONIES

The Tall Tale Town went haggard
& poopt its pants
when the Korean Moon
stript to dance

He dropt his Messiah shawl
& bought a wharf –
He did a shimmy & a dip
splitting the Town in half

the Money Moonies cropt
His flag around the Town
opened his Freebee Treasury
as it froze into a frown

the Mayor hugged the Tube
armed in dragon skin –
he was the first to sniff the Plague
now the Nation's following him

the Lemming Moon is the Voice
of communal ownership
with servants, echoes, & digits
relishing the Master's trip

He pays a fine & heady price
for any form of fish
& the local boats kowtow to the cash
from THE CHURCH of the WITCH

The Town is gaga & googoo
as the Moonies retrench –
the Town's almost in their pocket
gagging on the Money stench

the Sky Court has a docket
on these cronies of a Thief –
their days are shadowed
& their Faith is under the Ax of Grief

the Town is still uptight
& scared to the gills –
the pickets barbwire the New One
as a placard or a meeting kills

the 5 Aces of the Potato Moon
flood the Blessing of the Fleet –
ah the fruitcake & salty tournament
grinning at the Town's defeat

The Town aint dead yet
though locked in fishball combat –
God & Country's going after them
& who can ante that

Belief is finally at Stake
& anyone's as good as Gold –
these 2 are never divided
unless you lose your hold

so hop to the jamboree of Death
& watch Moonarchy fumble down
as the rising Sunnies
relight a benighted Town!

Let us drum upon your sounding board, it is better than ersatz entertainment, this real theatre.

July 8/1981

Khambaty, alone, stood the onslaught

Only one man on the City Council had the tenacity and stamina, foresight and wisdom of persecution on his side, and he stood up against the wolf of fear and hysteria, the kittens pussyfooting on the hot bare wires: Ab Khambaty came through that conclave of firecrackers and impolite duelling, alone!

A lighthouse on the social tempest in Fishtown, a milling beacon against Councilor Foote's analysis of the conquest of Gloucester by the Moonies. Foote, in this instance, a cause of glaucoma, knight by the dark demons, to bring Khambaty down.

O how the participators swayed to the proponents and opponents, their emotions, the drum of the speakers.

As I said in the aisle of the City Hall chamber of debates and lawmaking, since we live in a society of buy and sell, how can you prevent people from purchasing property on the waterfront and anywhere else?

And Carolyn O'Connor, after hesitating noticeably, perhaps thinking of the next election, voted meekly with that majority, the easy way out.

Khambaty and a few from the audience had to stand the onslaughts of Wayne Morgan, the pastor from Pigeon Cove, the research reverend, and my dear friend from Magnolia, Frances Leary, yet Khambaty stayed by his principles. He did not weaken nor fumble.

Gloucester vs. the Moonies, a typical foolishness, headed by wrongway Leo Alper, the city bookkeeper, suddenly launched into international notoriety tackling Pope John Paul to save Gloucester from an invading religious sect: the Demogorgon in the eyes of the local local. You'd think some citizens had a knowledge span of 50 years. And Alper, a Jew, who should know better.

The usual case of too much heat, not enough light.

And the Gloucester Daily Times refusing to take ads from this so-called menace. The Times succumbing to the provincial lobotomy. Our newspaper buckled under demagoguery. I cannot believe it.

Khambaty, you stay remembered forever, for that lonely position among the councilors during Gloucester's dark night of imaginary fear, which some who cannot smile at, who self-terrorized as they are, might soon be able to.

Holy Catfish, if the Moonies sweep Gloucester into their coffers, the Vatican's next, is that it?

At the speed Alper's hacking it, he'll make Gloucester the farce of America.

Dont be hobgoblins of infamy, turn this whole affair into the comedy it is, challenge the Moonies with the Sunnies, create Mister irreverent SUN, and have a ball.

July 14/1981

ps/

Those who fear brainwashing are most insecure at home.

Parents who raise children to think for themselves have the least worry, they expose them to all religions, trusting them to see the good and bad in each of the institutions.

Before Adam Smith, before Karl Marx, before Supply side, before Capital, before Labor, before Union, there was St. Augustine, who said:

Find out how much God has given you,
and from it take what you need;
the remainder which you do not
require is needed by others.
The superfluities of the rich
are the necessities of the poor.
Those who retain what is superfluous
possess the goods of others.

I think I once saw that carved on the gravestone of a quarryman in a cemetery on the side of a hill of the setting sun.

August 5th/1981

When self-interest is the bone of gnawing and we learn where that bone comes from, we have second thoughts, sometimes third, about that activity, which is a poor meat, even for sharpening teeth at the expense of the real ground of being, if the free market is the sine qua non of our money motivating society, than we had better be freer with innovations, if that is possible, maybe with social, self-interest, ah, here's something that is lost sight of, such as profit sharing fully, which some enlightened business men are acutely aware of and doing something about it, small as it may be, and more of this would take the edge off all the fat teeth, instead of plugging the ear-waves and the eyesights with that cracked record, desperately chewing at that famous bone, the alpha omega of bite bite ambition, wherewith monomania, egomania, and megalomania, the most intense and disturbed forms of self absorption that endanger self and society, that cannot hear or see the heartbeat of the common world, for all things and peoples are inter-related, second thoughts could be about the human marrow in that bone whatever color, creed, gender, or national origin, O Yes, we have our Movie Hero, and his stage is the whole world, too bad he's punch drunk in the ninth round of his role in his stringy ring of rickety bones, and so onward to the evils of self interest, destroy the environment and its inhabitants in the process, have a good time at it as the rich are, and plot to become a millionaire, and then live handsomely, dont ever take this religious incentive away from us, it's the only reason for living anyway, ask any renowned model of this miraculous opportunity, check the prisons while you're at it, and the madhouses with iron windows, and those at large, and watch Ray-gun with his bulldog Haig round up the unemployed youths and shove them into the armies to die in old men's wars to save their dysfunctioning society, ah limited nuclear skirmishes, the mightiest giant of them all is tippling tizzy and ready to blast the earth off its orbit for almighty self interest

November 12/1981

This is an open suggestion to married & unmarried lovers:

When you are in those moments of divinities, think of sending your sweeping flood tides of the Heart into and over the unloved and unloving, the destroyers of Nature, the polluters of the local environment, because lovers are closest to the bodies of Love, animals, flowers, vegetables, minerals, fishes, & birds.

Let that be the Aftermath!

The power is with Lovers, who dont need or want it, but who have never exercised it enough

& the miracle we are in, becomes the Earth's!

If this is the wildest of dreams, I'm living in, you are considering it, anything is possible.

December 19/1981

The globe is roasting

The globe is roasting with the sacred and profane imperialisms.

Pity poor Polanski, religion promises the rewards and punishments of the next life, and the Party, the benefits of this, and both short change her, because the roots of the invisible are in the visible.

January 4/1982

There are some persons who are deaf
and their ears are full of Beethoven's breakers on
the red rocks, the stormy silences of strange
creations inside their skulls.

One or two who are blind and hold
galaxies of unseen senses behind their eyeballs,
hot with telling tales & a few have the patience to
hear, who witness their visions alone

Many are dumb with broken words,
combinations of sounds from the Mediterranean,
from the underside of childhood, who are tongue-
tied with all the inflections languages are heir to

Everyone carries a special kind of Night
inside a Spring

enduring a civil service Socialist economy
run by the Capitalist fuel, Dogma, tossing limited
white bread to the Unemployed and crumbs to the
poor and the homeless

January 6/1982

Have you thought about tinctures
about suggestions
& examples
about breaking new paths
& excellence in anything for its own sake

ah for one Centre
like an old unused school
given freely
to the citizens for multiple uses of the
functioning arts
where is the heart & mind of a City?

if we drop an inkling of a notion into our
heads as we fall asleep, we wake up acting on it
this is the night-route to the great Giver

January 13/1982

Vows of marriage, not war, needed

I throw this idea out for our readers to mull over.

How can we arrange to set the scene so that Russia and America could start courting each other?

Such a marriage could prevent a world Holocaust that would upset Hitler's wildest dream, for he aint dead yet.

How about a celebration to bring the Russian Woman and the American Man together, say in the Library of Congress or the Institute of Leninist Theory and Practice, or maybe some less pretentious place?

I am sure they will find a lot in common, besides politics.

She has the Socialism of Poverty, and he has bellyache Capitalist security.

So already you can see the attraction; it's a shame they should destroy each other before they have tasted Wedded Bliss.

Who knows, it could lead the way toward a resurrection of family life, and free love styles: What a surprise for Terra Firma!

You gotta believe it first, it is worth a try, start entertaining it, talk about it to your friends, sleep on it, play with the fun of it, it can unleash an Energy that would turn Big Atom's cheeks jaundiced with envy!

Such a thought can take over a tiny town, and one at a time, catch on like soulfire!

Can you see the eyes of that approaching Ikon, the heavenly couple!

Reagan could be best man, with Haig pulling his coat tails.

January 27/1982

Granpa Reagan is on the third rail by asking to dissolve the Government of these United Illusions, and suggesting the abolition of the Washington DC brand of the House of Representatives, the Senate, the Supreme Court, and all the officials from the President to the tributaries, and letting the States work out their self-sufficiencies down to the cities and towns, villages and hamlets and neighborhoods, and finally to the Individual, sticking all responsibilities with this Numero Uno, the ultimate figure, which is where the world is in, in the first place.

February 6/1982

Dear **MAENAD**:

Will you dare engage your raison d'etre with an opposing or differing view toward a fructifying intercourse?

My first proposition is that there is no split in Nature: that each individual self contains that Unity it is alienated from, and that alienation is perpetrated by a split consciousness.

My second proposition is that that state of mind has divided itself from the heart, namely that that cut is used as a weapon against itself and society.

My third proposition is you cannot fight Power with Power, female Power against male Power, that only perpetuates the unending unnecessary struggle, LOVE only can deal creatively with the schism by absorbing the other as the other, and each becoming the dance of 2, or more accurately the dance of 4.

The Narcissus mirror is a dead end, nothing dynamic can happen, there's no breakthrough into a new development with another force, masturbation is OK as a means of releasing tension but it excludes the other and the world.

My fourth proposition is that polarity can serve a purpose providing it is open ended, namely that the female struggle against the Patriarchy implies a Matriarchy, and the establishing of one power for another, and perpetuating the see-saw, one's up, the other's down, exchanging positions is a boring routine, and is Maenad a beach-head for war, the destruction of the Patriarchy? Is it a battle for total pollution of Nature as the states of governments are hell-bent upon, the centuries old territorial psycho-sexual, class structured endgames? Look around and you see everywhere who the victims of divide and conquer really are.

The final proposition for the time at hand is the transmutations of the seed, that that genius is the deepmost root of the mystery in relation to the ovary, and the music they make for each other in the Creation of the Cosmos.

My offering is that a new consciousness is being born, will Maenad allow it in, or keep it out? Maenad is on tap, will it open up this avant-garde theatre? Or do you need more time to flex the muscles of your Mind?

February 13/1982

"... hell-bent for planetary overkill"

One "view" of the extremes we are confronted with constantly, as Jean Knox Gibb's "Stop, before it is too late" has a cool precision, and her understanding of the Bully Boys' game of knock the chip off my shoulder if you dare, her short biography of the Atom, the courageous action of Mavroules, the equally bold handling of whose got the biggest madness by Tsongas, all this, and the spirit of the groundswell against Macho Reagan's conclusion that the Nuclear Freeze is for the pigeons, her essay, and others' alertness, give us the feedback we expand with, that the inexorable exigencies of History will unsaddle the paranoid officials of society from riding their scheming Juggernaut, misreaders of the Governed's temperature, gutting human resources, hell-bent for planetary overkill, yes sirree, Reagan is the castor oil for our constipated economic life, he is the nightmare of this great Experiment, and the grassroots of Peace, the finest kind, that avaricious self-preoccupation through this temporary White House inhabitant is going for bust.

Super Duper USA afraid of Russia, what a Farce, or is Karl Marx's idea "from each according to his ability and to each according to his need" that makes for the inferiority, or is it that these 2 monoliths have something deep in common and could work it out and dont, because the Socialists believe in their cause and we fear our origins?

So whose got the best Dream, because that's all we live by.

We have been witnesses to the one-upmanship of Lockjaw, and civilian prostration to the military-industrial psychosis is a jingo kamikaze.

The living Christ, the zen Buddha, and the enlightening woman, are haunting the streets of the disunited States of Being, if I read the Decades correctly, we, the woman in the man, the man in the woman, the 1776 "revolution in the minds of the people" are experiencing the birthpangs of a global consciousness in the 80s.

The Founding Cartographers of this New World meant just that, an infinite awareness of operating in the holy local, as every cell of our Soul is, humming the Song of it, in the Heart of Earth.

March 29/1982

Development plan endangers city's beauty

Watch Schernig and his sidekick, the $7,900,000, the tourist filet mignon, change irretrievably the character and the nature of Gloucester.

So we're a dirty peacock, and they hanker to dress us up in fancy, artificial clothing, these entrepreneurs see us as primed for plucking, and re-educating, and our Body of the Beautiful aching to be ravished by the Commercials.

So watch these money wolves fatten themselves on this immaculate mind-preserve.

Watch how our legislators Silva and Buell tarantella.

Watch every move of the game of Sell, for Gloucester will end up false, plastic, high-priced for the top middle class and the Rich, as they shove the working people into the dumps and under the wharves, to serve themselves first, and finally.

Watch the skyscraper sharks, McGrath, Sylva and Associates with their bullion bucks and silken bullwhips.

Watch our birth connections ransacked openly and surreptitiously.

If the citizens have no ideal for our real city, then Progress destroys, look anywhere, see the Deceptions of our physical climate, if we give up our eyes and ears, then we are truly lost.

Watch how easy it is to slaughter a season.

All this in the name of raising the economy off its back.

After the already shifting scene, this attack (on Stage Fort Park, Stacy Boulevard, the Fitz Hugh Lane House, Solomon Jacobs Park, and our Ten Pound jewel) is the first assault, and could be the fatal blow.

May 27/1982

Read at the City Council Meeting, June 16, 1982

The so-called HERITAGE PARK is a smokescreen, is blinds us from our tasks of taking care of the CITY JUST AS IT IS, we have enough problems getting by without squandering millions on fake frosting, when that money can go where it is badly needed.

We are constantly faced with the lopsided view, of not beholding the work at hand in the multiple senses, as a carpenter or plumber does, or the granite builders of a City, (imagine home, neighborhood, & community as a working Cathedral!) be not set on going for the Touristi pocketbook, the throwaway baubles and the lost balloon memories.

Two members on the Council raised this dead issue, and so we are dealing with a living death, so please listen and study with 3 dimensional eyes.

We're here again so that Schernig & Company wont throw their stale cheese cake at our faces for 300 years or more.

now:

SOMETHINGS WE LET ALONE --

1. Like not tampering with Georges Bank.
2. Like not finagling with the Spirit of the City
3. Like not sinking Ten Pound Island into the Bubbler mud.
4. The Fitz Hugh Lane House is not asking for frills.
5. Neither is the Solomon Jacobs Park.
6. All Stage Fort needs is simple necessities like bathroom facilities.
7. Sure dress up Stacy Boulevard, but dont change it, or add any yucky-muckkies.

again:

GO WITH THE LIBERATING SPIRIT.

Dont for the love of Gloucester make a whore of her.

ps/

The Council defeated 6-3 the motion by Benotti & Porter to reconsider the Project ...

Carey jumped on the broken down waggon

Reconsideration wise

That was a neat back-track for the Times after its initial, unequivocal support for the so-called Heritage Park; nice to read you chawing on your first thoughts after the people and the council spoke out.

The whole issue is very simple, and has nothing to do with "purism." Just a matter of doing the job, any job, right, for all concerned, and in the round time, past, present and future, keeping the aim on the present which makes the other pair.

So the Times' second thought is let us all gather around the table, and not let Schernig, et al, ram their project down our throats without our participation.

Two late wakers on the council have second thoughts, too, so pray they have three dimensional eyes.

Now think again, Times, dont we have enough problems taking care of the city as it is, such as the obvious task of keeping it clean, and no money to help doing it, except for certain citizens' personal feel for the community?

Why just washing, brushing, and seeding Stacy Boulevard is enough, as well as Stage Fort, with whatever is required for it to be more of itself, and with all those millions, spread it out for the custodians and caretakers, whose job will be to nurture our original condition, providing work for the maintenance crews, look, we did it.

Get the idea?

June 21/1982

United States of the Spirit!

The Dogtown Lyceum Futures Forum was an enactment of the Comedy of Mistakes only in reversed patterns of personal transcendence, thoroughly enjoyed by the participants, yet reflecting current codes of limited engagements.

Here is my Blue Print, starting with the PRESENT, which is perpetually Now.

Go for new social Horizons, move from the restrictions of Necessity to the liberties of the Untried overhauling the defunct monetary morality we have been cursed with, enduring the Minimum instead of Maximum private and public simultaneities for the common good.

The self, the family, and the community are in states of insulated chaos, when they begin to observe the underlying interconnections of natural unities, things will change as that unifying Vision transmutes Routine, and elevates the Human.

Here the means and ends for discovering the art of living and loving, that the public and private are interchangeable, that the more you give the more you get back, the less you offer the less returns, that to be satisfied with roles and ruts and the craving for material riches is a soul killer and a repetitious ennui.

How to separate local government from the national, and institute a new economic independence and emancipation? When the prime priority is the super buck, get it fast, but don't get busted, for that is the real sin.

Can Gloucester escape the inherited inequalities and invent a better game?

Yes, let us become sea-farers of the Whole, for we reap out of this adventure what we go after, or is being a parts people enough?

Let us look at what we have: Capitalism and Security at loggerheads. Big Biz with haphazard employment, the Welfare System badgered in quicklime, and Security with public occupations as police workers, fire workers, postal workers, etc.

I propose these other questions: Can we have full employment; can Gloucester become self-sufficient; can there be a future for our children here without traveling over the Cut or 128 and leaving altogether; will new Industry train and hire Gloucester people first; how much Economic Development can we handle, and not sink the ship?

My concrete suggestions are: for Business and Commerce to consider profit-sharing, which will benefit production and quality; Banks to cut their interest rates in half; change the philosophy of Education, aim at preparing students for the vocations of self-fulfillment wherein work and play are mutually inclusive, that polarized self hate and self love have their origins in individually split parents, in a schizoid civilization, yet head and heart are in one body, self and society in the same life; on this ground of relating, the evolving self can learn to stand alone secure, with or without another in the theatres of the purely creative.

Contemplate the four-day week; initiate retirement at 50, if that fits in with true values, making room for the oncoming generations; do an indepth study on the poverty of navigation.

Once this approach is under way we'll be experiencing individual whole health, as will the family and the city, starry stung at these never before used relationships really working.

The old incentives will be seen for what they were, exploiting and subverting matter and spirit against Cape Ann as a heartmind of the Cosmos.

The mortal and immortal are two sides of this primal reality that are never divided.

I say let us go for the ROOTS, and the trunk and branches will take care of themselves.

Hail the United States of the Spirit!

November 15/1982

Alive as any heart is . . .

Regina Cole's elegy of the '60s was sad indeed, she thinks the dream of the flower children has been aborted. That Dream never dies, it is a linear, circular evolution, generations change and grow up, they mature and become part of the Status Quo, even as some of the veterans of the counter-culture.

Many of us remember the 30s and the WPA, and the 40s radical labor movement that brought about Social Security under the Roosevelt Administration, a monumental capstone, and the McCarthy Reign of Hysteria in the 50s, all preparation for Vietnam, and the Mandala consciousness.

We know how Government and Politics control the Country's minds and materials, we know the constant struggle to exact a more equitable distribution of the Earth's goods is in Congress where the Laws are made, depending on who makes them for whom and for what reason, and we have been given instructions by our Primal Legislators.

The Flower Man having the Child in him, the Flower Woman having the Child in her, living the Vision of a world view through local action, enacting the heavenly Gospel which is the real Dream on Earth, what could be more creative?

The Faith in Justice is invincible, and an on-going process, to be repeated for each generation differently.

Look what's happening to the 80s and we aren't even in the middle of the decade what with all the Nuclear Warheads bristling on the horizon and underground.

The Dream is alive as any heart is.

June 29/1983

Help Put The World Together Again

The leaders of the polarized empires have abdicated their responsibilities.

America struck Hiroshima.

It struck Nagasaki.

A third strike and America is out.

Reagan believes in a "limited nuclear war" to win, and so does his fellow traveller, H-bombardier Teller, who just said, "it would be nothing to evacuate New York City in 24 hours." A brilliant, nutty scientist with papers to rescue 11,000,000 people under the mushroom!

Impeach President Reagan before he sticks his night-finger at the Button dreaming the longhorn cows are the evil Russians.

The Child's time is here, putting everyone in touch with the wonder that is everywhere present.

Can you see the children's crusade with women and men dismantling nuclear warheads in all countries, saving their futures and the planet's life: watching polarity's harmony of yes and no without guns and H-bombs.

Poor suffering Earth, tired of so much hatred and fear, religious and economic, ecstatic (as she is anyway as herself) in the miracle of nations risen above the Poverty of Spirit and Matter, discovering with delight, that *there's enough for everyone.*

December 6, 1983

THE NAVIGATORS

HAND'S BREATH

The hand in the brain first
the brain in the listening hand
equal do they sync together
concurrently making the weather

the splitters who thrive on the wound
pour acid in for roasting the taste –
labor is the rhythm in the song of the brain
survey any frame!

The callouses are the commanding grip
the hands' breathing tempering the heat
working as the fish do for the bread
& the dancing bed!

The hands' blood has its own mind
& the tongue a sweating dictionary
when speaking is a plumb line's go
living's the Poem we all know!

THE BELLE OF LEGISLATION

Carolyn O'Connor

The Naked Truth of the City Council
& her first mate, booming Gus, the Foote
of the fishes, they know, she no sell
out to the exploiters who blotch up Cape Annie's Face

Pilgrim Rock, the barque which is herself
against the Status Quack, the rabid shots
& the bilge, steady as her exploring ship
through yakking seas, the fogs, no maps, & shoals

with a sense of more than today's little peoples
the no voice, the do nothings who have no legs
for involvement except when property papers
are threatened, as they storm the legislative lags

Captain Conscience working for the Good News
sleeping with one eye open against the Nays

WENDY QUINONES

newsprint scribe

They feared you, O monolith of truth
& justice, because you tried to unionize
the GD Times, so they fired you, these trite
souls of small power who could not break your knees-
brave lady of living words, you have arrived
at being, the granite this island is -
the dark outlook inlook busy as
your veins are for working as you rivet
fact & fiction together or separate
them, & simply show the thunder & lightning
your quarry is made of, a fulcrum of right
& left is where you function at, looting
is your enemy, though concealed in matter
& spirit, you flush them out with your meter

THE VIRGIN PARCHMENT

Jonathan Bayliss

Master of the minutiae & mountains
your springs! Poppies & pansies beat
against your reek skull, & bait
the mind there, wary of Moon-teens
who attend your starred-coffin tappings
these real fairies who know you
showering you with stories & touchings, ya
O scribe of the Mind's virginity, what trippings
on voyages into this unmapped interior!

I hear the nor'easters around your living Rock
& in the heart of it a holy ire
banked for a goal date, as the furies rake
up acolytes, haunted by eyes whose secrecies
blink at the edge of delighting & freeing seers!

THE WHEEL

Ars Poetica

Nothing's given
only the jungle-
as the self is

a head full of broken windows
the body under quicksands
& a free mind

thunder of Zeus
as a song in the bones
& no enlightening

the dust of gunpowder
on the cellar floors
a congress of mixed birds in the attic

on arched Learning
Maxims of grinning Death -
graffiti hallelujahs

kicked out of homes
or exiled
the initiated trouble makers

one at a time
only
& naked sight

a wedding in a casket
the new born
comes out of-

the joys of spending
pure gold
each moment is

AT SEA

A bundle of cerebellum Angelina
Sanfilippo! Right out of Jehovah's belly!
It is the monkfish eaters who are loony,
here's chowder with a touch of tansy & barley!

Queen Ann's lace & lip juice for Georges Bank,
crude oil & fishes make an inky stew
that kills, Old Country is Novello's bake,
the cousins at Kitchens who transmute a sty!

The wives in the guts of the boats have speech
and a mind with the nose of a shark!
Words come easy, they are bread & spinach!
& they have tricks and rallies to shake
the town up, get its ears & turn it around!
Angelina, Novello, & the fishes reign!

THE CURLEW

Gidget & Bernie Amero

Grow together, impossible, & yet
not so, go it as you have to, on your own,
come what may, staking everything on
what is right for one can be the yeast
for two, each urging thru the sticky straits
solamente, & earning another as
the companion, & discovering intimacies
no risks barred, for this is how it is,
the moments brand new as what she says
he adds to, & no owning as a strap
for beating the other, trusting experience
for the lonely advances, then stripping
the negatives for this holy ambiance

one boat, one sea, one house, two times two for one
world exciting them, taking the spell on!

THE STEEPLE OF SAN PIETRO

Is a mast for a deck with a flag
collecting prayers & fins & feet
on the shoulders of the walking street

the festival of a fate for a fortune
sending messages to the groupie fishes
asking the Saint to spy out the hitches

the low & lean boats & the sunken draggers
the risking wharves of the good & lousy prices
& the rounds of up & down the deadly ices

about his shadow are the clowning ragamuffins
navigating flood ties of a mighty grease
for the headlines of an angel tease

the captains & deckhands on their voyages
go hi lining for his red bandana
busting a trip or winning a madonna's manana

so kneel to the power of this patron
& the blessing of the lottery
but remember what the lock is & who the key

THE QUALITY OF COMING & GOING

At times they are divided the two
skins, the sexual & the spiritual, sex
clings to the senses savoring the tie,
the other's alone with the alone, seeking
the unities, having the womb & the tomb
together, the eye of one is two eyes
of one, two is two, each hearing a timbrel
the strangest timing is making with ease
by itself, love is a figure in the mind
the heart is an oil for, & the genitals
are letters, commas, dashes, pauses of tales
each player is bidden by some command

ah the skins of the spirit & the flesh
air joins, & the world is a royal flush!

ABORIGINE

Jackie Ellis Jamieson

under Ax ages of land the Algonquins
are breathing with her buried arrow-heads
at Plum Cove, under Babson's gains come
by listening to primitive hoards!

She is a foot ahead on the path of deed
by words married to the stance of the real-
Times vanishing are in the marks of the dead
who do their work in the dark & rule!

fiery North is her partner & playmate-
two trees walking with sparrows in their hair
red dust on their eyelids, a river moat
between what tongues, civilization is a whore
spreading bad Venus & harpies, their stone look sees!

They are the Night the deep singing sows!

TERRITORIAL AGGRANDISEMENT

So the house is mine, the street, the neighborhood,
take a village, a beach, Main Street, or City Hall
after you've got this in the personal pit, hid
for showing, then go for Portugee Hill
or the whole town & mine it to the core,
go with words, or boss a slice of History –
add to garbage & Bubbler, forget the cure
& the theory of first settling, rue
the carpetbaggers & private ownership,
documents, cemetery, direct interests-
be the Authority on the hamlet's shape
or the Souvenir, or storekeeper of Rights

this is my Acre, when any laser wit
says it's his, stealing bugs you, you've lost weight!

O CYCLOTRON

Peter Anastas

The nights flood over you you are the dawn
listening to the hidden heart of matter
& mind, a magnet to minutiae, a dam
against Evil, & a hungry motor
of particles pi squaring the emotions
for a system the ion of Love never tried
with humans yet, who falter & tread
upon the poor & raise mooching kins

Accelerator of the process, you keep
a steady dynamo on particulars
for departures & arrivals this Cape
is a drug any navigator lays
his love on, who is bewitched as you are
talking fish, seaweed houses & bloody air!

THE RED HOUSE ON QUINDARO LAND

At 16th & Wilson Blvd
    sitting at the window of John Brown's forehead

        the ghost of McGrath
        pacing the floors of naked mind

            the body of Nelson
            pulling together the thunderbolts for a
            tomahawk of wrath

Mberi sucking in the lineaments of tenderness
for songs of reunifications

                as Catalpa Whitehead
                pruning the Yucca tree
                mothers creatures of the invisible

This house of the New Person
where the poem is cropped into ears
making more of

This House with the flesh of Black Cemetery
& returning eyes disarming
imperial robes, patches or loin mandalas
the walls & floors creaking under the soles of still
restless ghosts

This Red School House in the nuggets of wheat
with the looking & listening
& a name held only to clinch the communications
working thru wind
where our real homes are!

Ole Elk hear
how that hidden Master in the loneliness of each

hammers out
a fistful of words or a stream
saying:
this is the sum & Sun of it
eat & be fed
this is all of me
& only a morsel

This Whole House:
the female JOY of colors & sounds
excluding none

June 16/80

COMMUNAL KALEIDOSCOPE

A strange CAT is prowling the streets of the blood
stream, she has human eyes & a mortal beat
her name is anyone, everywoman's blade
everyman's talent, every child's bite
of real Fantasy, no one is left
out, each one counts & the reward is the Joy
an act well done gives, the soul's aloft
with others, the town's wealth is the jade
of unstopping art, not money, not fame
the City intoxicated with itself
because it has found its Voice, its beauty & form!
we'll match the peace tides & the revelling surf!

Each one is a star in the theatre
life is, & CAT has theme & theurgy!

SOUND QUARRY

S R Scotti

Listening, each cell, each plant, each animal
a branch, a pebble, a wind, a shadow, a
link of harmony, each is the mute mute of the mill
of making, this man has a key to, aha!

The cadence of postures & emotions,
the love-hate swamps & tell-tale signs
he's digging, schooled in children's missions
& other's hermetics & confidante of sins -

The Friar's the piano of the Community
his ear to the unconscious of the citizens -
his mind is the rhythm inching into
the ceremonies opening the love-zones!

The Holy Water is the heartpulse of Music
& he's the Instrument of the Mystique!

BELOW DECK

Stephen Moynahan

The sleuth is arriving from a three year snooze
tracking down boners of the City Council,
hitting the Editors faux pas & fast as a sneeze
at errors of the Developers, who can steal
the City's searchlight! & sometimes do –
placing his bets & striking hard, he's laying
the foundation for the royal seat one day
in that flat Tower with four steeples, lying
low, waits for a gap to make a civic point –
if he can juggle circumstances & play
it cool & straight, & control his punt
he'll oil the judging Chair & not have to plea –
he's banking his interest, the concern is high
& steadfast, a good dream's hot in his hay!

THE DEATH KNELL OF PSYCHIATRY

Shaman Shaun McNiff

In a rich sleep the deity of No Face
is amusing through the 3rd Eye of Creation
at the children of the parental Force
vomiting & swallowing soul secretion

In a white waking the No Name medicine man
has shed the 13 skins of himself -
he is the contagious heartbeat of the Moon
there he relinquished his life & it is safe

The wholly Other is deep into his own
sowing images in 3 places at once
with the dancing drum the blood is, the freeing On
the ills fly from, & the lamprey doctors wince -

O revel in the revelations, cut
the bosses out for the health of a cat!

IMMIGRANT PETREL

Elaine Wing

Hey, O sovereign Fitz Hugh Lane a tight wind
has settled here with solid skies & coves,
ochre earth, purple voyages, a wise One
of colors using her interior keys
for springing into bloom the vast empties
of a great perception sleeping in our hearts!

No words are needed only the finest ties,
the flesh of marsh air & streets, fishing hates
the false that stains the immoveable center –

O solitary shades!   The tones of Pigment's lust
for dancing!   This pink petrel of the Saints is
with the great Optimum of the first & the last!

Memory of action is emotion seen at rest
uncanny as Moonrise & Sunset roost!

AMERICA ONE: or the map of the country seen from underground

Steven Lillybeck

Moline, Illinois's here, a young taproot
starting from Fishtown to size up
the continent, checking the divorce & rot
in the brain, going for the hidden apt
between the female Whitman & the male
Dickinson abroad in the giberish States
that hunger in the Mind for more than a meal,
cash, products with built in death, quicklime stocks
& shitty arts in the navels of the highbrows
or the morphine for en masse, this wild cat's
stuck the thermometer in the Eagle's brew,
the dissident rebellion, & the senses of Keats -

Psyche's pushing him through her terrible middle
into America Two, Three, Four, & Five's immortal

PRIMAL LOVE

Joe Garland

Black Bess hermitage is one of your arms
as you embrace the City of fisher peoples
& your heart's the other, your one eye the aim's
foundling, balancing teachers & pupils

O fulcrum the town is a beggar for
grazing out upon Amerindian plains -
the white house of your mind without fear
is a sanctuary for Nature's plans

the City's groggy inside our slumberland
as you are, a sometimes outsider, peering in
to stewing classes, character outlined
by that beloved pair, Truth & Beauty, on

this island running you, our shipwreck souls,
for this Chaos, words, as your in-look sails!

THE ALCHEMIST

Michael McNamara

I

The family disintegrated in his lap's
ague as the pied pauper went astray
& derelict in bolted cities, his grass lips
at a brother's suicide, his tree
stunted, his own lawyer against a misdeed

famished for news, his eyes & ears a rabbit's,
measuring & finding himself short, a dude
hip to Scrooge & Hamlet, & the raw beat's
unrecognitions gnawing for Spring rain -

& then to reinhabit a life to the hurt's
rainbow, or wrestling booze & demons, a rune
resident in the coalbins of loves & hates

his gut's in his head, joie de vivre the acres -
the swinging door of the two theatres!

II

Because he steps backward he comes forward
a listener, he's onto the Law
of Love, inclusion as the freedom
against exclusion, the restricting lie
of self, prohibiting the creative other,
who has more is more, or the diminisher
of Nature's unrecognized author
each is! & the dramaturgy is for all to share
in, the least shining as the mightiest
chorus of the Creation, the medicine
is he because he digs himself out of the East
giving it all away, driven by the Song!

Look up at the nightsky, the round clear
singing, who is one & each of the Choir!

ROBERTA GIBB'S MARATHON

O humble, O first treader among
the monks of the track, & pushed aside
by sleeping timekeepers, an easy mingler
after the facts of self, the first seed
drunk on the Truths of accuracy,
beholden to that measurer by word
& action with the oars of the see-saw!

Working with center, securely wading
overhead, staking everything on the quest

so far back amid the leaves the trunk
of her black light electrifies the quick
& the dead

                    going after the Law's trinkets
& cachet, steadfast as the wealth of woven
Intuition, jogging through the jungle, weaving!

MARRIED SCIENCE

Dan Greenbaum

He's at the back of the blizzard with his hand
on the compass in a steam of North Atlantic sweat
secure as the lull of peace, a pulse of the heard
neck deep in foam & charts & rights, a sweet
warrior guiding resources to their habitat
in the townspeople, protector of sperm
& ovaries, a light carrier, loosely taut -
guardian of our prime places with book & spear
of prescriptions! as chlorophyl & cells
working for organic raptures, nothing
less than the Whole of it! This is the Soul's
fiesta underground & over, footnoting
& aware that this is the Divine, teaching
us through him to the rituals of touching!

PILOT

Angela Sanfilippo

This messenger from Sicily is our figurehead
& the prow to unknowing knowns, the bell buoy's
lonely premonitions who hears & is heard,
familiar with the stinks & ghosts of the boatyards

our angel of arrivals & departures, the helm
in the skies as the undertows of her listenings braid
faith, petitioning the sharks of Washington, her Hymn
the recognition fishes have singing with her brood!

How simple, her working words coming as snow,
            or rain
without the acid, no pocket hollering for moola -
as a ship's crew is one, so's the community's ruin
or windfall, charting the trips in the stocks of Maya

we love her, we fisher people, full of the heart
mind, golden spenders, & veterans of cool heat!

BRAHMA

Philip Saltonstall Weld

He's castle borne & daring, his pastimes
are sailing the Zodiac with trimarans
of his own hankering, no buddies, no teams
& he passed them all in several runs
with the bat of his brain, the Moxie, the terror
of the Atlantic, invincible
as the genius of the alps! The eyes of Taurus,
wings of the heart, & the furnace of that bull!

ah to straddle the Atlantic alone
& to ride her! A mosquito & a giant
swallow in one, dream bitten, in a line
of ocean orgasm, a Poseidon joint!

Like the texture of a soul, a barque!
A mariner whose front is his back!

LIFE AFTER DEATH

Harry Martin

What reverence you have for the ghostly great -
it works in the bowels of your Africa!
Yr light rays reaching the sleepers & the awake
tie together these regions at the core

you are a bridge between these holy makers
& the readers, a current between
both endings & beginnings, mimicry
is your signature as you twine
a music for the eyes only! O magician
of gestures, stoops, profiles, live colors &
the single center of a whole navigation!
where they end you begin the circle on!

Author's bookworm! Priest of letters & images
on Main Street tracking down mirages!

ANGELUS

Lena Novello

How is it gardening a family
in the belly of a boat, landlocked,
sailing through hurricanes, ice winters, low
pressures of the primordial lack -

a wife of fishes, a mother of ocean
a cutting voice & mind in City Hall
against the ignorant weather, ancient
walls, bad blood, juggling Heaven & Hell

land too, is an unpredictable seas
for this wife & sister of citizens,
nurturer of the communal laughter, the sighs
& cries of loving in the untapped zones

the town is her household, her kitchen's the town's
breaking the barrier of the public private tunes!

WHERE WISHING COMES FROM

Annie Scholefield Thomas

It was behind a bar of story tellers
I first saw the estate of your future
hip deep among the watchers & the toilers
not around now, of a fetching & a fetcher
swimming as minnows, blue fishes, & shadows
that 2 hearts heard one sound of 2 bells
that held a double trinity shod with
news equal to the language of the ballet's
blood heaven,
            2 mirrors are about you now
& a third moulting a miracle in the night
listening to the marshes & what they know
of the creek's keepings, & the unsent note -

Putting it together creating daily
epiphanies around the pivot's dial!

ODE FOR SURVIVAL

in the lonely night our hearts cannot sleep
our minds are buoys in a nor'easter
dreaming on the seas' floors with the dead
the fish haunts & the children in our veins
some 179 ships out of once a harbor full
the unborn pulling at our elbows
the eelgrasses & beaches tugging for our concerns
the fishing grounds in our blood pulse
a grave bearded, stubborn people with testament
eye-rays

we are the clouds & the angles of waiting
we are the amoeba & the molecules & the atoms of the
Sun's delightings

we are the E Pluribus Unum soup
we are the feather friends & their unheard cryings
we are the amputated survivors of other coasts
'beware of the under-oil fall up
there are no dumb animals
the sea is our savior'

we are the blizzard gulls of glowtown
who carry these tenements & houses in their
meditations

loafing in the slants of the really found
our gizzards revelling as they do
            hugging our vessels homeward

& will we have to buy them
or let them rot in the memories of tables without fishes
these arrivals of liberty
familiar with the bodies of mountain winds & raving
            waters
their flights our innermost cells know in this
            ironhearted occupation

away with thinking astigmatism
we are the hope of submarine species
the trust of the cormorants & sandpipers
the prayers of the rounding rituals of Moonscapes
the Ma marshes of the infants
& the nearness of the whitegold re-sorcering
the roots of our city are in the sea!

Would you hack us apart
o floundering Republic
Georges Bank is our bread-basket
we are not dispensable
we are what we are
a fisherfolk
holy local

& we have instructing examples to go by
like blazing down the Atlantic shelf
up the Potomac River & into debating Congress!

October 26, 27, 1979

THE SEDUCTION OF MAGIC

Crash myth, crash symbol, crash mask, & the tales
that derail the process of the single eye
the I each carries alone, with all the tools
for setting down a house, an anchor, a
vista of the Vision behind the Seen -

kill roles & rotes & the hamster track
the mush the masses melt in & sewn
by Death's needle for the Master Trick -

did you live or were you just a pawn
for the Game you had nothing to do with -
whether you were or werent around, just wait
others are yourself who arent your pleasure & pain -

the one infinite & miniscule ride
not ridden, or wowie breaking thru the charade!

CORRESPONDENCES

The slave & the master have one habitat

who swap places now you know where you are at

AN ARISTOCRAT OF GENTILITY

Niel Lovisco, 1900-1981

First a dead silence then the whirring wings -
his breath took off & left behind a dove
trembling in the rooms, circling around little things
still alive, alighting on the shoulders of his love

in the body of that bird is the family
the friends who still hear the purr
of his lookings, the cool feathers of a devotee
truly human, his webbed fix on us, the hushed stirring
of his quieting calm, a stillness in the cooing sits
inside us, that other us, we cannot see
that sense that there is no separation outwits
us till we catch this flight of you & me

As we are in him so is he in us, this dove he is
we are the shadow of when ours companion his

FISHER WOMAN: Peg Sibley

City Hall on bowspirit, mast, & full
bosom! A woman sloop on bicycle &
podium! A tongue quick as bursting foam
ocean salt, swift as wave on wave in
one moiling mind few bards can dally with
let alone parry, a cool fire enemies
flee from, or warm themselves at, ah what
blooming zest only the wildest storms amaze
as she does, her family ahead & behind
her, mistress & master of her Barque
on pavement, rally, dock, a regal hound
in cloud county! The living letters of her Book!

All writ, & still writing as each second is
expanding a seed, bud, fruit, of eyes!

The JUDITH LEE ROSE

The Jesus, Joseph & Mary of the fleet
lies between sand & hot beds in a casket
of hell encounters, endurance & fishes fluting
by & inhabiting the log of the costly
Chances

the old talk encrusted with barnacles,
the spy-glasses of the family in the Captain's
Crus cabinet, at the nets the raw knuckles
white as fish bones, the far off Cape turns
with shades of the ruminating left
at home

here's relief of the prayer beads
Jesus Joseph & Mary listening lift
the burdens for the on coming extra bids

the rewards of reverses & new titles
of the Human forging ahead as turtles

CHARLES BIANCHINI

1912-1981

He wont weigh a piece of granite in his hand
again but he is the granite, he wont measure a line
he is the unseen line, he wont look at a lane
again he is the lane, O the silences honed
him well for he wont gaze out to sea
again he is the sea, he wont be at
her elbow again, he's in her heartbeat, his sons saw
as he looks out of their eyes, now this is it,
the life of the quarry, the house, the views,
he is about in the trees, the paths, & the weather's
works who stood in beauty as a simple vase
does, & in motion as the ways of the waters

he is silent as his garden presides
with her breathing him who is absent & present

DUENDE

Donna O'Sullivan

The silences of deep waters being sewed
through big fog, little holes opening the Eye
in the abyss of You we are, the one sod
the Mind is, unminding the tribal ore
& the Chorus of cells serving the cell -
A mothering ship of the God & the Goddess
of energies, the individual seal
each breaks illuminating the goading -

Fire mountain's dancing on the drum of
her signals, robed with patterns of unspoken
arrivals & departures granting If -

Aha, by unction of entering, spunking
the accoutrements of the Negative, reviving
& fleshing the Spirit of the unheard voices

MISTRESS OF THE SEAS

Sylvia Swartz Cohen 1923-1981

You were in the heart of human storms, so how
could it be otherwise that a blizzard should
take you, O Bright Side soul, to hoe
elsewhere your family lore, a quiet shade
among the living, as you fished with the finest
kind pushing life forward, still among
us, as you were before, as much as you have furnished
lovers! so there is no ending, we mingle
in so many levels Song has yet to catch
up with, even as the oncoming billows
saying, the promise is here, go & coach
one another as we do revelling, our bellows
gonging in you, she in us, look up at the staring
stars, O they are clicking in each one steering!

INSTINCT ARCHITECTURE

Kirk Noyes

Property, bank accounts, & steady jobs,
this is the real estate, lacking any
or all of these, the unreal position jabs
the exile, the city's foreign, ennui
is an old dog sniffing for a tall crony -

silence and language in food and shelter
covering the nakedness, nook and cranny
possessing sprite collateral & shoals, too -

there is no mortgage for words & pure writing
Spirit has no substance for any bank
& yet without them everything turns rotten
the digits, numbers, dollar signs in the book

words as words go with the oxygen
whose wealth is as vital as the androgyne

A GOOD HARBOR TALE

It was a winter morning of straits
when the tide was flattening out of sight
the blue windstorm lifted
my Inca hat
& rolled it a whirling black hoop
windbelled & speeding
for the water alps
I raced after it
as it engined onward
hot for the foam chowder
twice I almost nailed it
when the bursting pearl surf took it on
I waited for the breakers to toss it back
but it loved tumbling with the green surges
I was standing in a water-color feeling
had my 2 heads missing my beloved
dived for the first sea of her
Salt Island filming the scene
I went for my rubber boots
my car had flung a belt
which held me to one deed at a time
veering back to the cutting winds again
on that white wet sahara beach
I spotted a roosting gull
which I thought could be my singing totem

mad horses still
chomping at Parnassus rumbling
when that dark bird turned into a caved-in
mosque
the stove dried the impatience out
the salt stiffened the cone
it sits riveted
at home listening to the approaching
body of her Atlantic

THE WATERS OF THE WORD

Where words between persons lose their meanings
no longer inform the gut, are held as cheap
as weeds, for living waters that cannot chirp
go dry & dusty, & so do the morning's
humans have auras, so does the common ground
of Earth, & when these thin out, ignored
by irreverence lack a bloodmind, we groan
as One, mortally ill, a final first need
is yelling, that what we rarely give a second
thought to, is urgent, the simple things
we lost belief in, nor given thanks
for, seeing interconnections, seasoned
by poverty of anomie, time's broken vase,
that water is the living blood of our views

THE SEA SALT

Phil Salzman

So we have a mountain of folklife right
in the gem box!
                              The catalyzing Rock
engineering the active art of the root!

A hasid dancer on the ocean wrack,
the foam, the windspume & rich salt,
the band, the urchins, the parents, & the news-

who is the sky's lore & the pregant silt!

His festival is our family & his acute nose
the writer of the Spirit's newspaper!

We've just begun to turn the City inside
out, he's the drumstick, guitar, & piper
of the music at the heart of sea & sod!

As the many in his one sounding pearl's
history, directed by a different pulse!

CHARLEY LOWE, revealing TIME

1932-1981

The map of the City was in his mind & now
underground & in the air for others
to see as his words did straight & new
for he was a renegade at obeying orders
against the truth of things as they are
& he had X ray talk a confidante of timing -
his camera is a blind eye now teeming
with news few live with, lie with, or
stumble upon, as he is cruising in his black
box with the roots of vision coming
out of our eyes when we do see, or block
it out, or stay with him as he is combing
the byways & intimate views of fish-town
unseen & hearing uninterruptedly the tune

TREE MEDIUM

Teresa McGarrity

Fishnet of light on the Ocean floor
your rootlets are thrilling the stars with eyes that go
through you, each phosphorescent flair
transmitting flower juices! A devoted jinn
of liberating charities. Gypsy wire,
wizard youth of events, & wraith sower
of Numbers no claquing Devil's war
can smear, stain, overthrow you or sour!

You go about owning nothing & no
address, & everything is provided -

A walking Tree at the centre of the New
Earth!

The desert lives through you & Voodoo!

Main Street is your kitchen & alley ways
your viands are talismans transmuting woes!

THE CATCH

A stone
thrown
in the well
has all
that water

BREAKING THE WORLD EGG ONE BY ONE

It is always me and mine, I say we & ours!
This is the day the Infant cries out loud
for the Joy this Entrance is, & the heirs
singing who is the Child we are led
by, who is the Mind & Matter, Delight
cannot have enough with! Who is whispering
each of us is eternal, forget the loot
that divides us as we kowtow to the wrong
deeds, this Child sitting on the Nukes
has broken through the crust of the petrified
Vision, thundering against the feud
that alienates is the music that unites!

The lotus in the Egg we are the petals of,
this egg the eye is, all the clouds peeled off!

MAENAD

Paula Estey

You have seized your left-hand place as the Goddess
& by mind & passion undermined the Male
who is all Male, this unbalanced & goady
Destroyer of Nature, this split off mule
of himself's tenderness, that you are whole
will help him rescue the female inside
him, nothing less than the overturn of his Hill!

Furrow, wet, weed, & shove in your seed
of relatedness into his Heart's head!

Out of you He came out of him you will come -
the Song of It, the new creatures will heed!

Seeing things as they are in the Honeycomb!

To be equal to that generator
of the Miracles, this hiding Twin tour!

DOROTHY CAHILL's

manifesto against nuclear murder

A battleground of Good & Evil is
your body, 2 ideas without a table
between them except your bones & thinking as
the grit they masticate, the salt of trouble
spicing a dull time Imagination
is incapable of applying itself to-

Wars & pestilence & sovereignty nurture
the strict machine humans exist for, the die
is life is wasted on people

the mean
they settle on is so below the mettle
of the Mind's outlook, the me & mine
first, denying the given, Heaven's model!

The begetter destroys the begotten –
the Earth is waiting for the Child's begetting!

BELOVED COUNTRY

There is a chill of rigor mortis in the air
as the Monuments at the marrow, that a nation
cannot see the poverty of the spirit, or
is waiting to live on the song of the original notion!

Terrible is the death of a young civilization
& heart breaking to be helpless & blind
are the roots to be watered again with blood
to heat the vessels of the outlawed Legend?

Behold the Oligarchies of Decay legislating evils
into the molecules of Economy, strapping mettle
& the Changes, become like the glass-eyed idols
of dead life, cities & towns servant to a clay model

O marry the Word to the Action for a see & be seen
the real Republic is a citizen's resurrection!

NATIVE GRANITE

William Edward McNamara 1909-1980

A crab apple tree with a child's heart
& born to saw & hammer, pruning & plowing
who built his house with tongue of freezing heat
reared his kids in a boiler's brew by plying
ships' intestines, his leather voice
crackled by the fracas of arguments
& kickback degrees, & surviving, vex
affection, recalling spit-word commands,
working to the hilt he left a gnarled estate
his heirs divided on the precipice -
he hated carpetbagger & upstart,
a wise acre no one can now oppose

his dear tools are scattered as the handiwork
he's the oxygen for the lights of his wick

⌐MPASS

A lone
while gull
on a riot
sea
sitting
still
on the peaks
& pits

THE FEMININE PRINCIPLE

Paul Pallazola

His feet are with treeroots his hair in the skies
& in his gut the city throbbing night by day
changing locks on the laws to even the scores
between the classes clarifying the die

the underdog's to meet the competition
as an equal as the sexes fathom Nature's -
the meaning of his work has his whole attention
as the lost details & the goal he nurtures

consumed by the innate beauty of Justice
& the flaws in the conditioned appetite -
his mind a companion to present jesus
sucking an elan of the Moon tit
fortified by the subterranean juices
a One guiding him by what the ancients taught

THE TOWN'S GUILT

On a ragbag curtain the face appears
the foreigner with pin-point eyes of light
& a beard, speaking in a silence alert
to how we are, at peace, as Ignorance pours
acid rain on the skins of the innocent,
his eyelight turning that water into salt
& bread each of us the body of that Saint
in a partitioned death, being sold
down the shekel sewer every hour
of Cash & Credit, every picture of debt
the chained role of the Buyer & the Whore
each in that figure, & the mouth is full of dirt,
yet the Conscience is a white diamond look
saying in any one of you I leak

WATER TALKS

I am the Spirit of the Water
I am H2O
I can be split
but not killed
without me people, animals, flowers, insects, germs
molecules and atoms die
the grasses shrink and sink out of sight
the trees get arteriosclerosis
branches fall off
trunks turn to stoned fossils

I am the sister of brother Air
Clouds are my mother Moon's
predawn moistures & mists & fogs
are messengers of cornucopias
If you and your parents have no interest in me
the blood dries up between us
your houses are separated from other homes
Yet you all live off my one water
do you love living as much as I do
then be as One to caring for the one ground
we are the creatures of
as I am for any number of ones as you are One
Then my Spirit is in you
& I know it
so will you
& we will never be separated again

Your plenty will be mine
there's a drought in the souls of the citizens
There is no division between
sky & sea & land
there is no split between water & blood
there is no separation between light & darkness
drought is an absence of innermost seeing
the cell & the galaxy are opposite ends
            of the same center
drought is a state of thinking
a condition of alienation
drought is a sickness in the body of the city
as our Island is a living soul
so is the Earth
& the life source is water
drought is taking me for granted
so ravish me at your peril

I love living
do you
Then show me

O little children
lead us
for you hear & see things just as they are
you are the carriers of my Spirit
the bloodsong of this astonishing existence!

CHARLEY OLSON

the son

A burnt house among others, rebuilding it
with this own hands, & with the help of a few
friends lifted it upon a ground cloud at
the Head of the Harbor, for his far
site deep in living!
                                        The Father of him
self!
        The Mother of his new land fishing
the two ends of a genealogy at home!

His palms' palimpsest, the designer's fusion
of perception & instinct as the mark
of his private dig
                                        the City's feel
is in his ore, & the original make
of it fired by the communal fuel

Born alone, & attending to the core's
delineation, hewing at his cares

NANCY GOODMAN'S DOGTOWN CALENDAR

I have a memory of a time when my
family had each of us & other families
feasting & singing around a giant May
pole table in City Hall making Laws!

I remember a dream of marble streets
& open houses, rioting waterfronts
when Money was free for covering straits
& a drunken Moon set the town in a frenzy!

I could see Ambition & First Love spreading
itself, the light of never the same again -
when Trust was a golden penny sprouting
Sexual Laughter, & backbiting an exiled goon -

It was an Age when everyone owned a piece
of the Town, & each one a Mayor setting the pace!

DEBORAH GOODWIN & HISTORY

One drop of Aqua Vitae on an iron
door, a suffocating cellar, & a rigid board
room for the arrival of the alien onion!

The glint of an odd eye, a 60s beard
& the castaway anchor still tied to the Past-
the windows opening the special hours
for the mode of Today as the cousin pest
at home with her inventions & her oars

the sense of the art bizarre is on tap
the bulletin is aching to do a pirouette
on the streets of the Museum, her tape
is running the Wedding of the incoming It
with the outgoing had enought still on
display, & quietly her spinning's in

THE GHOST OF ROCKY NECK

Jack Clarke

The poem is bareass & a wave of stratosphere
daring Love to be, or flash dreams gutter
out as dead mills have lost their solar fire
& lack of shelter is the local goiter

this Mona Lisa man, living both ends
at once, a Venus on the half shell
of the harvest song, the action of Id's
genii, this warrior without a shield!

Being in many places as a hub is
all the spoken stay at periphery
& center few have the wheel whirring as
he does, even when loyalists go awry

the wraith of our harbor peninsula
watching how naked words & seedlings lay!

MASSEUSE MIDWIFE

Kate Boyle

The gradients of the soul & the flesh
are a music you are attuned to, when
you massaged my aura with flashing
eelgrasses caressing me, bearing my wind
body down a stream to the middle of the earth
where I hit a bonfire that erupted me
in a cascade of seeds that falling back ate
the soil for dancing!
Your triumph for my
second life, as a womb nourishes a secret
so do your hands & words wiping away
projected ills the self's accepted, the sacred
Temple is restored for the I of we!

O medicine midwife of the unifying dreaming
each is locked in deciphering the drama

CAPT'N BILL SIBLEY'S TALE

1919-1983

The night he laid down to sleep a fish saw
him & two tears of joy fell upon his face -
his life was fuller than anyone could see
so the Ocean called back its brother force -

strange death that is not a taking away
but giving! The forsythias love him, winter
trumps Him & he wins with a joker! We
are his solitaire, something else wants him!

He's left no one behind, look at his Mate
& the five stark characters making more!
What a family has sprung out of our might!
That smile loaded with the wealth we admire!

Day & night are one as he is, nothing's
missing, he's caught the fish we are noting!

THE IMMACULATE CONCEPTION OF

Joel Scholefield

You are open to where the God is concerned
a high liner of the human deeps
fishing in Gotham & the ultra sinned
out with the meta meta who adapts
to the navel voyagers, the one Truth
of Loving suffusing your holy cells!
Going with the unexpected is your treat!
Neutral to confessions the family seals
friendships that are more kin for experiments
you fear not, the oval delivery
of Education for Love & Leisure, & mounds
for manifestations of dream ray

sower by actions in other hamlets
a child look in the background of homilies

the thunder in my head

I, too, in the lightning of later, see
early intuitions of immortality
right in the center of a Being that is mine
& thine
wondering why the eyes that cannot see
like that hidden tree
that hears what we cannot hear
rooted in two worlds
are at home as the Cosmos hurls
in a million places
& each one interfaces!
The same seen tree
with life & death at either end
storing them apart & together
as the enemy in the friend –
all this is ourself is the holy weather
seldom seen
& heavy behind the green!
O how the shadows play in the light
& another living in the Night!

NEW BLOOD

James Munn

Point man to the town & custodian of streets
ten years up to your hips & finally at home
speaking as anyone of us who bows & struts
on little stages, an impresario or ham –
You have the sidewalks & a platform in Newsmount
goosing bad habits & patriot politics –
the welfare & double dealings tax
your schedules, arete & excrement
work in household & community as twins
you are a Father to, & perhaps one day
be a Mayor for, for you are a dawn
man in deeds, using the image as it turns
the trick for the processes of excellence
employing gut feelings, Mind & lance!

AIR'S THEATRE

Sheila Ferrini

There are parts that turns the quick
of a player to a celestial blaze
& both are fused against the quack
of dont meddle with the Social as the blues
& reds go yellow forging a truth
changing the looking hearers to a gem
they rarely see, lifted from a frozen troth
of Artifice, wallow in a jam
that's a white sugar for blood's engine,
or the Stage is throbbing a personal present
as you are a martyr or in Joy
caught by the vicissitudes of prescience

Exploring the character of the voicer
as you do, an uninhibited visa

PASSPORT

I

It starts at intimate correspondences
by a glance, a mad action, a touch outre
taken in as Love is, or choke in a siege
of cracked lens, side-tracked, missing true
emotion, prejudging is the yardstick
that backfires, & the recipient devours
a dry remorse & tenants a stock
stew, till eaten, hungering for better views

label another & you fit your frame
there's more than meets the eye or hearing –
the obvious is a stale bread, dead ends come from
as being openly aware & you're on
& in! Whatever's going's going as
you are I am, & this is how it is

2

Drop the rags, peel off the lint from up
tight household, skim the fat off the iris,
the Soul is naked, do you need the Op
Ed page when you are wholly Eros
O Psyche! If there are better places let
me know, as I am It's instrument
so are you at the edges as you delete
yourself & you are new, you mount, I mount!

This is the work, you are being done to, you
are doing it, the world's all yours, you are
the world, the personal pores are open, yeah,
& Ecstacy is the elusive air
we are exchanging no one owns & each
is free with giving & taking the Witch's hatch!

ENGINEER OF SONG

Felipe Weld, Secundo

So far in he's all out, this despot
of the heart, Lady Neptune in touch
with the unforgettable, the soul sounding poet
of the new It, & underwater torching
the black in each for the mystic combination
gone whole hog as he is!

Quietly spinning
as a seed does savoring the nurture
freed by itself & hailing the other spanning
the Janus abyss!
One string symphony,
a blue horn, doing the precognition
by, this is me goddamit, if you dont know
eureka, ask!
Risk impulse & the notion!

in love with the world he is pregnant with
playing the communal dark house for all its worth!

a few words nodding under the compost of night
muck!
                                        O Inertia, beloved of idle
Mind among the masses of neuters
at either end of the tape worm

                                                    Id
potters scampering with golden missiles & rainbow
Deaths
                    Joy for any action
                                                    what moral /
                                                                    things
are perfect just as they go
                                                    imbue
us with ointments & incense, speaking with Tongues
the spectacle is the Pome, the pulp of Song
& anything you can get away with,
                                                                lay
with Illusions
                                        what differences does it assign
the same goes on inside a truth or a lie
Variations on the Theme of Avarice
Art's banker
                                        & the canker in the sunrise

THE WISH FULFILLING GEM

Betty Smith

As the heart is so is the City for her
an expanding Garden, her concerns
for watering, weeding, pruning what's Here
& Now, a common seer at the scenes
of politics & paradise-

                                        her blood
throbbing against injustice &
the defamation of Beauty, a hot blade
for exorcizing Demon dividend
from the Enterprize of the heuristic work!

Agent of the angels, her jutting brow
taking on the blizzards, her mind's wick
flaming inside the opal she is, brewing
ichor & moly the town's half awake
on, in the back of a celestial breeding!

A DAIMON

Paul Hamilton

Before the Map & tours, the Zodiac
of animal Id enjoying the human head,
the Deathhold, the senses with Spirit ichor
waiting with Love's abundance & hid

O forearms & fists of pure energy
working though Dreams the Mind is unaware
of, bestowing a surreal jive
of monumental forms, Imagination's war
against dead systems, inspiring deeds
above & beyond the routine reach,
this triumph that says nothing dies
only Changes for the greater range -

wood, metal, stone, any matter have God figures
you create with them dissolving our fatigues!

DYNAMITE, POW WOW

for Christopher Lee Thomas

With his blocks I build a fortress of my own
with a sweep of his arm he breaks it down
I try his slide & he yells out no no
Vincent, why why I ask & he with a grave din
it's too big for you using me for his looks'
measuring rod against his Pow Wow world
as we lasooed the roaring tides of white bullocks!
He ponders on the sounding off of words
as he stores them in his incredible bank!
With his Parents & me at the opposite end
of the spectrum, he's in charge of 3 books
without owning them! This 2 year old India!

Let it fall in in the rites of entertaining
O Siva be trusting as he with his timing!

October 23, 1983

THE SECRET EAR

of Bob Callahan

Where did he arise from, he came from a story
his mother heard from his father, his father
picked up from the Unicorn who drinks Fate
at the Well of the Moon! A star-bard
throwing seeds on the shores of a Listening
that is hungry for the selfless food
found with deluxe daring of the Feminine
tribes on the alert, who uncannily confide!

What is this that is changing the atmosphere
with a word, a nod, a gesture, a tap,
a note from a flute, we've never been here before!

Hearing the Unknown, anyone can with a tip
of tongue seized with the transmission of it –
the Tale of where the Spoken & Heard is at!

IMPECCCABLE WARRIOR

Paul Kenyon 1907-1983

Taking no sides & being the fulcrum
between them, handling the facts with fair
weather, no pretense, a brother of field crane
& chronometer, stoking his banked fire

the holiness of the Job he attended
that the servant & the master share
equal rites as upon a tintype
they have come from at sea to the shore

if the whole is seen the particular
blazes on its own, so the mind is free
enjoying itself covering the lure
of the assignment, the wrangle & the fray

distances were the trade marks of his concern
as he gave it all to whatever scene

,N'S BARK

Ramona Murray

. the compost of the past is a museum
of apparition loving intrigues & mayhem

her steeple is tuned into the Divine
& memory's meditating on the weathervane

the river's rounding the garden of the soul
introducing angels for her mental ceiling

there are always two to find out about
in the womb of the ocean love is baiting

the treasure's in the lap of the anonymous -
who's king on the cat's back but the seagreen mouse

I'm the world that the Cosmos is ignoring
yet dead I'm alive, we are both noted

master mariner of interior journeys
spreading news of the attendant Genius

LAUGHING IRON Speaks With Davia Jenkins

You are in the possession of your life
& loves, the hungry man of your voice
scampers with the little lady of your laugh,
star-meat & sunlight is your visa!

No one is over you, & your pace
is an intensity quiet as ebb
tale, flush with giving away the password
to celebrating the innermost orbit!

Time kneels to you, so do the rollers on your breasts
the winds licking your ankles, the askance
observers timid & satisfied with brass –
what conflict is burning beneath the looking skins

O captain, first mate, crew, & lonely tide
from the underseas of your beatitude!

THE TAKEN

Paul Sawyer

Fishing for souls in Berkeley with the contagion
of loving by words in action where the poem
is!
            Anything less is off at a tangent -
O non-violent posture & head of Pan

Countries are Lourdes of money on the make
with & mostly without, you stride in power
using the sages, educating the meek
for the transfiguration of the Poor
in Spirit & bread!

            You've deciphered the Book
of Finalities & joined the disciples
bringing the Hereafter!

            The eagle & the buck
are learning & following your examples!

Few believe it, It has chosen us
clear as the blood where the singing is!

WHERE MOMENTS ARE

Harry Wheeler 1911-1983

The little talks, Harry, the pitch of a view
& you'd jump into the other world
then, where you are listening & nothing is vague
even as you hung & hang onto a word
savoring it before the flood of them
came & took us under, remember, Harry
the way of the mind's lust for meaning, the theme
of capturing the essence & be in no hurry
with the action, loving our vocabulary!

all the books of the library are in your head
now, so keep talking, I am oggling, O'Leary
is questioning, you are going at it hot
& accurate, among the tongues, Harry, hearing
the sound of definitions not for hiring!

HEART'S GUINNESS

Kevin Ellis

On the summit of Wall Street, a prince
of vistas, & carpenter to Christ

comrade to angles & spirals, oranges & prunes,
mostly alone in his underworld cruise

he wakes up a Buddha in my Garden
a pin wheel to madman Dionysius

or working for a Shakespearean gadfly
walking on ideas in windy shoes

his bed the blessed words of his Lady
who's making bread with the eelgrass of his soul

there is no Art for him only Life's ladder
in his belly, his silo, & his sail

Air is eternal as personal breath
& intercourse Scriptures, people are his broth!

THE CHART

The City Council has a brown paper bag
of rusty tools & a manual
for order, as it sleeps & plods in a bog -

theory & practice is the goal of all
but each goes according to the law
of itself, & Maximus avoids the crowd
ambling by himself wrapped with low
clouds on the water streets, the slippery creed
of Perception, the town is a foghorn
of Mammon, as the Council with blind folders
& an oath attached to Blackburn's lost fingers
dictates an I O U to the center fielders

Governing is always left to others
for others, dividing inners from outers

KATHLEEN MURRAY's Invisible Eye

You are me & I am you, all the senses
hungry for what the soul is full of, what
Earth is saying, I am you, you are seeing
the unseen powers of our present wit!

Going West for your East, my East in your West
being the music color & form is making
& putting to use destruction & waste
as lessons for winning the mocking market -
inebriant pith of the noticing spheres
around us, & caretaker of details -
timing is our gnosis as the surf's
Essene is the essence of our tools!

A pillar of light & spirit lust
familiar of the looking among the least

RICH POOR WATERFRONT

Sarah Robbins

The harbor is the address of the far
off seas, & though full of clouds & storms
it is clean as thunder, an open affair
of arrivals, departures, communal steams

bilge is taboo as the sewer outlets
that stink & clots the eelgrass & rainbow hair
the house of no walls for the easy loots,
a co-operative workshop, or the riff-raff of a whore

O she is teaching us to become ocean
gardeners, immersed over her brow
washing the dumped-on creatures, airing
flora news drowning in the scum brew

her senses reflecting the healing water
the harbor is, origin of the City's weather

OPENING THE NIGHT

(CAT's out & in & on its own)

From seedlings on a bed of hi protein
loam, above & below, mad flowers pop
anywhere on this ocean Rock, a wild tune
of home actors smoking a holy pipe!

As complete & fine as the aroma
of the uplifting surprise of the blossoms –
the impossible as the condemned rumor
arrived!
The singing steel of blue sons
& daughters, the Present as the theatre
of the triple living!
The gut's gold, & no
lacking of triumph as the New
local old as the sea's naked utter!

What's lacking
or to hog for, it's all
here, subtle as our mystery oil!

ONYX MESSENGER

Marilynn Bever

Ever see the gene in the twinkle of a glance
that held prophecies coming on for a notion
of the greatest good so easily igniting
the fun of excellence?
                                        That people are
better than computers but only artists
of living surpass them -
                                        this either/or
when both is the luck of the Ur truths!

If the brain is the King of the Third Temple
on the wrong rail, & the heart is the Queen
sabotaged by one proposition, team
work is full of maggots devouring the quintessence

There's little to show for the invisible quantum
games you are overthrowing tombs with!

BASE-BALL

The Characters

Al	Edward Price
Helen	Ann Koumou
Maureen	Christina Thibodeau
Developer #1	John Hart
Developer #2	Genny Linsky
Developer #3	Susan Bulba
Developer #4	Judd Wilson, Jr
Mayor	Tim Perkins
Pickets	Eva Sklar
	Michael McNamara
	Tracy Tinkham

Directed by Michael McNamara
Co-produced by Michael McNamara and Genny Linsky.

First performed September 28, 29, 30 and October 1st, 1983 at the Blackburn Tavern, Gloucester, Massachusetts. The first scene being omitted.

First Scene: a ballet of a forgotten communal rite

The characters of the play run into the stage dancing in a free for all, a wild chaos, to the distant drum of a steady beating, one tries climbing up a wall, another is tripping on a bersek involvement with himself, another is letting all his organs fly out of his body, one is having problems with her hair, two others have trouble getting their bodies to melt into the rhythms of the individual collective, one is trying to arrest his shadow, each being drawn to one central figure, the young woman, slowly merging, (one by one according to an inner metamorphosis) around her, intuitively magnetized by her, each being pulled toward her and away, separately galvanizing around her, forming a plant, they kneel in a circle and all together bending backwards, chanting WOMB, the sound that comes out of fishes, & she a human pistil, whirling in a delirium of Joy, slowly falling to her knees, becoming a golden glowing resonant wombing Song, the humming behind the phenomena of Nature, the undersea FLOWER.

The action can take as long as the actors are playing out their parts for making the lotus.

Second Scene opens with Al Morey, the speculator, & Helen Babson Morey, his wife

Al	The President's anthem has been heard in all the States of Ambition & you are stone deaf
Helen	The song wrong as this marriage unfolding the estrangement
Al	O, a refined flagellator or in your attic a masturbating bride of Christ
Helen	Fighting's been our intimate friction
Al	Ever since you got greedy with your land I want to build with it & you shrink it even as you shut me out of your body's future, our land!
Helen	My father's foresight for the island he revered he sees what is going on from where he is –

He left acres of it for the family
& for the town he loved dearly
even as he is underground
listening to the opposing camps
he is alone in me
as the name is
& I will battle to the last inch of my
flesh
& the last breath of my brain
against the desecrations
& despoilers!
He has eyes as round as the earth is!
Dead he is Nature alive
which is pure light
separate & together
impossible to divide,
because everything behind
the pupils of the eyes is clairvoyant
for the Black there
does see
as he does through me
a voice of the Great Spirit watching
every one is making
& that light cannot be killed!

Al What a Fall Out
beauty & ugliness go together

separate them
and monotony waylays us all

Helen You cannot see as I do
I cannot see as you
My father loaned this land
for the living to nourish
& to care for
in sickness & in health
in life & in death

Al Why do you cart in the hieroglyphics
of the marriage scriptures

Helen because it is the same tissue of
parchment
the land's my body
& I'm not selling it down the sewer
to pile up green paper in the bank

Al You call money, paper?!

Helen Compared to this land
it's a donkey's wind

Al My God in Hell
no wonder we cant make it
in bed anymore
we're miles apart in the head
& the body is a shadow between us

Helen Our values are back to back

Al	Why didnt I see this in you before
Helen	Because most men think with their roosters
Al	A hard hat that's what you are
Helen	Then you've made me what I am
Al	Dont give me that ointment Time just rubs off the veneer & exposes the stuff that's imbedded within
Helen	Exactly I'm for the island's ways & you are for making money off it
Al	Build for today There's no tomorrow only today! Tomorrow I wont be around Frig the Future
Helen	Destruction of the environment which is his body his eyelight is seeing after death through me

Al Cockeyed woman
living his death
pure spirit crap
& you want to go back to farming?

Helen & Fishing!

Al Back to Nature?!

Helen Al, that's all there is!
It's no going backward
It's getting the eyes to see through
things as they desire to be seen

Al & they have a mind as we do
Jesus Mary
you're reversing everything –
That mind of yours
never stops
does it?!
You're trying to make a
woman out of me
Well, you're not going
to puncture the eyes of my balls!
No siree!

(A loud knock from outside, a man leaps, hands forward, reaching for a figure he sees, no one else does)

1st Man Got you this time –
after hunting the streets for jobs
I've got an arm of one!
Right on my mother's land
in my father's factory

Al (*to Helen*) He's going to be the Boss of the New
Building on the Waterfront

(Al gives her a brutal shove & she drops to the floor, her hand protecting her wrath, as another man jets into the room and lands on the other arm of the invisible figure)

2nd Man At last
off the Welfare Scrooge

Al (*to Helen*) See
these are the sons of a city
that cant provide
& I'm coming through for them!
Money's a self generator
& land left idle is a tax burden
a horse collar around our throats
do you hear!

(Another man busts in & grabs the waist of the invisible figure)

3rd Man Right around the gizzard
a hot shit
a job as good as a running river

1st Man Get off me!
(Nudging 3rd Man)

2nd Man You asshole
give me air!

(A 4th man leaps in)

4th Man I got your windpipe
& I'm gonna dictate the terms
because I'm the Union
no President will ever bust!

Al (*kicking at him*)
A shit head!

(The 4th Man whacks Al at the shanks as Al topples on the four of them, they scramble, each trying to wrestle down the invisible figure)

Al Where's the son of a bitch
hiding

1st Man In that lady there

3rd Man Yeah, in her head

4th Man In her woman's hood!

Al *(pushing them aside to free himself of them)*

The jobs are not in her
They're in my Frigate on the Water!
You first vision!
May some angel help you
to bring it to port
But the Devil's your Banker
& He's out to beat us all –

(staring at Helen)

How did I ever
marry you

1st Man *(shoving Al off them)*

It's the eyes I'm after

4th Man I've got the head

(showing it in both hands)

1st Man *(trying to take it away from him)*

Fuck off you hornblower!

3rd Man *(grabbing the head away & lifting it high)*

hi ya hoe!
hi ya he!

(the others pounce on him)

Oh no you dont

(he dances around with it as the three flit around him, he bucking them off)

He's our man
we've got the beacon of Dogtown
the humping quarries
the map of the home wrecks
& the EDICT of the Developers!

1st Man Let me hold it
I want to feel
the song in its head

Helen It's made of straw!

1st Man Give it, give, give it!
I've never made it to the top
Please, one touch
& I'll know it's real!

3rd Man *(tossing it to the 1st Man)*
Only for as long as a leaf falls!

1st Man *(ecstatic)*
It's the light my parents
never saw!
It's the rainbow all in one pot!

2nd Man Me too
let me look into its eyes!

3rd Man You cant
it's pure black!

(1st Man throwing it to the 2nd Man)

2nd Man 2 pupils in 2 seas!
& I'm the Hero in it
listen
It's telling me I'm gonna be a
millionaire
I'll be the buddy of the Buddha!

Al *(rushing to see for himself)*
You're playing
with an Illusion!

Helen Another vision!

Al Been idle too long
You've been sucking off
the Government tit
& giving nothing back
guzzle, guzzle
the taxes of the successful
do you hear
you potheads?!

1st Man Right & dead wrong!

3rd Man Lookee!
(Hoists the head up high again & sings)
I'm the Mayor
with the Golden Key
I'm the Vault of Cape Ann Bank &
Trust
I'm the Emperor of Greenbacks!

2nd Man My Turn
My Turn!

(3rd Man tosses it to him, who stares at the eyes)

Tiger eyes!
Forest eyes!
My lady's eyes!
My unborn children's eyes!

4th Man Me! Me! Me!

(2nd Man tosses it to him, & he too is mesmerized by the head)

One eye is my father's!
The other my mother's!
& there are two
movies of them
running together
always apart
& I cannot hear a word
only the messages of their signs
& gestures
& they are yelling, cursing
& fighting in bed
& my heart is trembling between them!

3rd Man Let me look!

4th Man You cant
you dont have my eyes to

(He cuddles the head & pulls away from them into himself & Al, angered & frustrated comes down on his arm with both hands.)

Al You dope fiend!

4th Man You bastard
I've dropped the head

(They scramble for it & in the tussle Al jumps backward)

3rd Man Murderer!
(He kneels down at the head)
May your crummy soul
drink the River Styx forever!
O it's crushed

2nd Man Can it see?

3rd Man Nothing in the skull of it
where have the eyes gone?

4th Man There!

(They look toward Al, he turns away & steps on the eyes)

The Men Together
O! O! O!
You blind son of a whore!

(Pickets enter & walk around the men with placards)

Picket We are striking
against the trouble makers
the enemies of Progress!

(Pickets chant the placard slogans, making the V sign with two fingers)

BUILD FOR TODAY

THERE'S NO TOMORROW
ONLY TODAY

TOMORROW I WONT BE AROUND

A CADILLAC FOR EACH
OVER-ACHIEVER

IF YOU ARE NOT A MILLIONAIRE,
IT'S YOUR OWN FAULT

Pickets You can eat the scenery
Down with parasite families
on Welfare
ME FIRST!
UP YOURS!

(They trot around in a ring twice, & the lasso of the pickets corral the Men, and Al is thrown bodily out of their hoop, falling at Helen's feet. They hobble off leaving Helen & Al alone.)

Helen They've broken your bones?

Al Like hell they have
a few dents & bruises

but my head is safe
& my mind is inexorably set!

Helen Against me

Al A half yes
& a half no

Helen You're a sneaky player, Alfred
But I'm as fixed in my position
as you are
And you're not going to industrialize
my Father's Body
not as long as I'm upright
& kicking
& underground our law
will guard our heritage
the name stays
& its loyalties to a greater trust
than you can ever understand!

Al *(rubbing his ankles and thighs)*
I cant live as a kept husband!
My manhood's at stake!

Helen What's that on your sole?

Al What soul?

Helen The sole of your shoe!

Al *(sizing it)*
Eyesplatter!

Helen It has a light life!

Al Eyeshit!

Helen That's it
that's the core of our differences
& you said it
no truer words every sprung
from your lips

Al You're singing in the fog

Helen It's all around us
spilling over into the water supply
the quarries
even the springs are gutted with it
& who knows everything about
groundwater

Al Beating the old refrain
with a new stanza

Helen Sometimes the old pettifoggers
spit the truth out
as children do
& you did

Al I put my ass in my mouth

Helen Just as good
you cant hear yourself
as I can

and the word that describes the Chaos
popped out

Al Come off it
Cut the mystery

Helen Right again
turned inside out!

Al You're back at our courtship
when Joy was our audience

Helen & did whatever we did
but we lost the trick of keeping it alive

Al the children brought us down to earth!
As the day's work did

Helen And need not have interrupted it
Alfred, cant you see –
with one word you shamed
all the benefits of the pursuit of
happiness
the First Fathers gave us the clue to,
everyone is exploiting

Al Come off
that song & dance

Helen You said it again
working can be a singing & dancing!
We are lost in our private lives
& the private is public!

Al A quicksand
You're into words
you're back into courting

Helen Again you've said it
Alfred, you dont hear yourself
& I'm trying to help you hear
as I hear you –
Life is a form of continual courting!
Its the heart of the mystery
& to go against it
is what you have on your sole
underneath the lowest part of you
where you called it
EYESHIT!
The turds of your ego!
Can you hear
now!?

Al But shitting is the act of Nature!
I do it
You do it
so you have your eye back
Are you happy now!

Helen Folly's fool
you missed it –

Al So do you
& that's why

we cannot see
eye to eye

Helen & no light between us
for carrying my body to you
& yours to me
& through each other
standing together in a pure
illumination
as we did in our honeymooning

Al So life is a honeymoon –
you're heading backwards
to the looneybin!

Helen Alfred
manure is a fertilizer
but when the human eyelight shits
it destroys the very land it lives off
& pollutes the sea around it
as the land is
so are we
as we are
so is the land
the earth is a solitary human being
or at each stage
each one is!

Al Too female for me –
so I'm a dumb bastard

a brute in your eyes –
if you take over
with your Earth-Mother pacifism
we'll be vassals of the enemy
who wants what we have
& I aint sharing mine

Helen Vessels for each other –
& light was our boundless energy –
We are getting older & decaying
because we interfere with its joyous
activities!
Cut off from the springs
all we have left between us
is my Father's legacy
& you are not going to over run it
with you metal monsters!

Al Dont be so cocksure

Helen Because I am
you wont undo me
or my ancestors!

(Al barges her with his shoulder)

Al Female prick!

(She loses her balance & falls over as he tears at her dress)

Cat to cat!
You're more appetizing now

than you ever were

(thru his teeth)

& my lightning's
gonna strike!

(He rips off her clothes & rapes her as she is screaming, the light goes out.)

(Lights on, revealing Helen dishevelled & on her side sobbing, Al is on his belly, without his pants, as 1st Man enters & the 4th Man who appraises the scene.)

1st Man WHO do you think won?

4th Man Looks like neither

1st Man He's the payola

4th Man She's with the kids

1st Man We're the soup

4th Man & they're knocked out in sleep
& dreaming

1st Man The eyes are out –
Like the ones he crushed
with an accidental step

(The 1st Man takes a rag & throws it over Al, as the 4th Man pulls Helen's dream dress over her thighs.)

1st Man Neither's dead

4th Man Might as well be by the shapes
they're in!

1st Man Dont forget man
he's for us

4th Man & she's against –
I aint buying that!

1st Man It's the fucking scene
For & Against
Get it!?

4th Man Nah,
How can you be
For & Against
at the same time
It's where the opposites
meet

1st Man Then where are we
We dont have that going for us

4th Man Not on the surface
but underneath it all
we do
Like you want a Job
& I grab for the titty?

1st Man Uncle Sammy's wife's

4th Man Dont care whose it is

1st Man You're gonna be a beat kid

4th Man looking up at the coffin's lid

1st Man with dead eyes!

4th Man I wont be around then

1st Man So you're in the Government's casket
with a blank vision

4th Man & silver glasses

1st Man You see out of
& we cant see in!

(The figures of Al & Helen are stirring, hearing them, keeping still, taking it all in.)

4th Man Just like these two
fucked out birds!

1st Man Stoned like the land
she's got a death grip on –
what good is it idle?

4th Man What was it the Bible said
about flowers & birds and beasts

1st Man something like they dont labor
& Nature provides for them

4th Man Like a Chinese Vase with peacock turds
in it, huh

1st Man May be for all I know

4th Man Hey, maybe Scriptural Incense

1st Man For a half wit plumber
you swim in pretty deep waters!
You ever step in a house off the street
& notice what pigpens some people
wallow in

4th Man Some are so spick & span
their razors cut you

1st Man I've been in most of the bathrooms
you can read their characters there!

4th Man As a home is so is the community
at loggerheads
look at the garbage
drowning out the drink

1st Man So save it
with a skyscraper of Free Enterprize

Al (*poking Helen in the ribs & shouting into her ear*)
Get that, Old Lady

1st Man They're coming to

4th Man You're telling me people are donkeys

1st Man Yeah, stupid & ignorant
many go crawling on their guts
like worms do

4th Man That's because their eyes
are squashed out
This guy's done it
with his unthinking boot

(Al grabs his leg & bites it)

O, you fucking rattlesnake!

(struggling to free himself)

Let go, you stinking viper!

(punching Al in his backside & getting loose)

Let's shove off

1st Man I'm hanging on
& seeing it thru

(He strolls toward Helen, looking down at her, summing her up, she clutches his ankle and sinks her teeth in it, as he screams.)

O bloody murderer
you mad-dog!

(violently shaking her off, he flees)

Al You got him instead
of me

You & your goddamn high falutin
ideas of yourself
& those walleyed citizens
all of them out there

(he waves his arm over the audience & back in)

You think they are of one mind
they're so addled
paddled & floundering
adding 2 & 3
they come up with 8 different figures

(Helen covers her ears)

You're like them
the 3 monkeys
no see no hear no talkie
Just so much junk in the way of
Progress
if we didnt design Jobs for them
they'd eat us out of house & bank
A voracious water-serpent your people
are –
3 monkeys in one woman!

Helen A monster, that's what you are
out of your human senses
flailing away at windmills
a rhino who's plundering body & soul

as you'll do the earth in
& one time I loved you
still married to this about face

Al We are all joined in law
or out of law
look at those libbers on the loose
even animals dont mate like they do
hogging off the City Compound
with or without husbands
One horny lover after the other
like tenants & strangers in a bordello
parasites on the backs of the taxpayers
dogs & cats are more civilized
& this is your Park Reservation Status
Keep off the Precious Drink
to support their free life styles –
& who's a mad dog?
Who?
You!
You bit that man
with your bear trap!
High on a mad song!

(Maureen rushes in, she's in a blouse & silk skirt)

Maureen Dad!

(Seeing her mother on the floor in disarray)

Mother!

(Kneeling beside her)

What does this mean?

(Looking up at Al)

Al Now, now, Maureen
dont jump to conclusions –
Your mother & I
have been acting out
a little play of our own
& you're carried away
on circumstantial evidence

(Maureen questioning)

Maureen & it's none of my business

Al Yes

Helen No

Al No

Helen Yes

Al You're too young for this game

Helen Of Hard Ball

Maureen Mother?!

Al A simple disagreement
Maureen
nothing to cloud your pretty eyes with!

Helen An out of hand
encounter, huh?

Al Another edge of the serious
I'd say

(Maureen helping her mother collect herself)

Maureen I'm seeing more than
you are giving me credit for –
I'm a new woman

Al I can see
Maureen
we've just had a quarrel
some people lock it inside
we did
but it burst out by itself
& we are the better for it
Huh, Helen?

Helen It was a low game
& you think it's even
so we can breathe a bit

Al It's easier now

Maureen I dont feel right
something's nagging inside me
you're both not letting me in

Al Maureen, dont push it -
another time & place

Helen He's for Skyscrapers on the Watershed
& I'm for KEEP OUT of my Father's
inheritance
for the Community's survival

Maureen & that's a difference
to break a family apart for?
(Al turning away from them)
Is it true, Daddy?

Al We were into hardball
she said it
before we knew what ate us

Helen 2 opposing ideas
have trouble in the same household

Al Somethings we have no control over -
one is the beast lurking
about in the dark bushes of our
unknown selves
& spring at us
making us their puppets

Maureen & it's in me, too?

Al It's sleeping or poking around
in each one of us

Maureen I've seen its face in nightmares
sometimes it has your brooding look
when I cant reach you
when I desperately hunger
for supporting affection

Helen I went to my father
anytime for anything
he was always there
like the Sun at night
I never had a better friend

Al like a high mound in a valley
& no ugly billboards

Helen Yes, we had our thunderclouds
& their music

Al How idyllic . . .

Maureen Mother was lucky

Helen & now the pits

Al Because you're ever rigid
you wont flow with the changes
you're an iron Past
you're in your father's dead life

Helen He is all about us
he's in everything growing
that has space to
outside of your cement civilization

Maureen I never heard you talk like this before

Al Because we grow up
& I'm fighting her for Community
Survival
& you're in the flush of a rosebud

Helen Community destruction
get that camera in focus!
go backward a few moments
before Maureen got slapped in the face
with a bad scene
& look again
from here –
Your past which is your Future
I will never be a party to –

Al You have been
you are
you always will be
married to me
or divorced

Helen Divorced as we are in marriage

Maureen Am I wooden bridge
between you two –
I'm beginning to see how weak it is
almost like nothing
a wisp of some cloud
you both made

& the wind is taking away

Al Maureen, dear child . . .

Maureen You said I am a woman
in blossoms

Al It hasnt been easy lately

Helen We are at the edge
& on the rocks

Maureen Is that what you cant tell me?

Al It's not that final, Maureen
Nothing ever is

Helen A wrong decision is

Al It can be changed
or reversed

Helen like a rape . . .
of the land

Maureen Mother?!
It is not possible

Helen Anything is -
even in the house of royalty
it happens
even in Church
It's man tripping on
his ugliest power

people cant bear
too much reality
not even you, my dear

Maureen O not in my home

Al Dont let your mind
run away with you
Dont jump into disaster

Helen Let her jump
with her two feet on the ground
standing upright
like any daughter has to
armed to the teeth
with the facts . . .
nothing less!

Al So it's a war to the death?

Maureen O no!

Helen O yes
that's the way you've chosen

Al & no compromising

Helen not with principles . . .
never!

Al See, Maureen
she gives it a name
sets the place

& the terms of the warfare

Helen Dont let him divide you
with that smoke-screen
It's a deadly weapon

Al O no, the law of Nature

Helen A foul strategy
to destroy & succeed –
what he did to me
he will do to the landscape
the fertile undersoil
& to . . . you

Al Goddamn your cheek

(He slaps her across the mouth)

Maureen Oh!

(Sucking in her breath in horror, as Helen withdraws, stung to the quick)

Al I've had enough!

(He leaves & to Maureen)

Help her
if you can

(Maureen shouldering her mother)

Maureen It's the end

Helen Not yet
I stung him

& the truth boiling
in his gut
sprung out

Maureen No No!

Helen O Yes!
It's the beast in the man
Divine or evil
Some know -
they are angels
some dont
they are devils -
This is the contest
each of them has to endure

Maureen & we encourage
one or the other

Helen You're a quick learner
My ancestors are proud of you

Maureen How was it at first
with you, Mother?

Helen He was an angel
then

Maureen Today the Devil has him
why do they swing to their opposites

Helen Some balance them

Maureen & Dad's polarized

Helen Because he cant see me
as I am –
only as I mirror the image
in his head

Maureen & his heart?

Helen is in his head

Maureen & you dont make love
like you used to

Helen Yes, Maureen, we dont –
we live too much in the head these
years –
Earth & Heaven have no bridge
no home
& no bed

Maureen Will it be the same with me?

Helen Different & similar
or you could become a magician
& have love as often as you want it
& as many of them
& live indefinitely
There's more going on
than your parents have to show
or offer you
as you grow older
you get familiar with persons you never
paid attention to before

becoming a friend to flowers
& castaways

Maureen like I'm living your life
& you are living mine

Helen We are both present to
the same life
a first love with the world
we lose with our innocence –
I know a man
whose life is a poem
not in any book
dancing on his hands
as Nature does
up-side-down
in-side-out
who is intoxicated
minding the varieties of loving
& he has a way of awakening
that song in me too
but when he's gone
that song in me
is a Nun in a lonely place

Maureen & in me
I am searching for an angel
& it is sleeping in Dad
Mother
I love you

Helen I love you, too, Maureen

(They embrace as Al comes in)

Al A private tea party, huh

Helen You could join
but your heart's knotted

Al So you think I'm ready
for open surgery

Helen Only you know that

(The 4 Men walk in as a delegation)

1st Man Mr. Morey
we are a one industry Town
Fishing is a sport
for unsteady people
who fish in the Summer
& fuck in the Winter
sucking off City Hall nipples

2nd Man Our last hope
is kaleidoscope employment

Helen Who invited you

2nd Man Al Morey
our father who art on earth

Helen He did?

(She pierces Al with her questioning appraisal)

4th Man Ask him

Al In troubled times
we take drastic measures

Helen You will strip me again
& in front of these flunkeys

Al You gave me no leeway

1st Man The Law is on our side

2nd Man Financiers, Madam
not floozies

3rd Man of the Corporate City

4th Man of the Fishing Future

1st Man What we cant take by hook

2nd Man or crook

3rd Man we pull the rug out
of indolence

4th Man from under your Genealogy

1st Man & take by eminent domain

Al The last recourse Providence
has supplied us –
Nature recycles itself
so if we alter it
it comes back in another
form & power
nothing is really

destroyed!
This is the Process of Creation
& you go with it

Helen Over my dead body!

Al It's you
against the rights of the Community
& you are alone
& isolated –
I'm the Moral of the Majority!

Helen Your numbers are a hollow myth –
The beginning began with One
& that One includes me
& the whole City's in me
because my fathers are underground!

Al A mindset of asphalt
Reason is knocking itself silly again
& my business is
breaking grounds of the New
Developments

Helen Your road will undermine
the destination I am!
Where my fathers are
so am I!

Al You haggle us to extremes –
you'll be lucky to find yourself
a footnote in the history books

(The Men throw a blanket over her and cart her frantic, struggling, figure out.)

Maureen *(attacking her father)*

Daddy, you cant do this
to mother!

Al Take it easy, dear –
She's also my pigheaded wife
(holding her in the vise of his arms)
she wont come to any harm –
we're just locking her up
till we get Law of the City Council
running

Maureen Where are you taking her?
What are those goons doing to her?
(Maureen breaks loose)

Al Now, now
she's forced our hand
to take over the whole shebang
including her Body
which is the head of her Ancestors
But our Land too!
& half of mine by Marriage!

Maureen Yours?!

Al As you are my daughter
& hers

the result of our together
the One you make of us both –
So is her property
half mine by Marriage!

Maureen You are robbing Mother
of herself
& stealing the ancestral land
you cannot do that –
I'm going to the police

Al It wont help Helen,
we're on a speeding train

(She runs to exit, he blocks it, she claws at him, they grapple against each other, she turning into a wild cat)

You're my daughter
& my property

(In the bitter struggle, he tears off her blouse, her breasts are aghast & provocative, Al is overcome by the excitement, they wrestle falling down, she is yelling bloody murder, he pins her down.)

& mine
by family domain!

(He rapes her, the lights go out, her sobbing & crying is heard. Lights out)

(Lights on, the 4 Developers in high collar white shirts with pearl stick-

pins, one or two with sleeves rolled up their forearms, with Al & the Mayor, who is chewing on a dead cigar, taking turns throwing the dice, they are facing the audience.)

Al This for unity
(throwing dice)

1st Developer Out –
What is this dance

Mayor Gimme those cat eyes

4th Developer Calico Man

2nd Developer Lucky cucumba

Mayor (*blowing on dice*)
Ever see cats eyes on stilts
or watch 'em in your alleys?

3rd Developer He's our tomato Man
Hot on numbas

2nd Developer Looka that form!

Mayor (*tossing the dice upward as they clink*)
A double square 8!

2nd Developer What's the choice –
Fort Square
for Condos!

Mayor Window on the Harbor!
(throwing again)
A King's View!

1st Developer A lame six

(picking up the dice & handing them to the Mayor)

Come on now
Crack the dark open!

2nd Developer Jesus spitting on all the imps of Hell
& the Crusaders storming City Hall

Mayor Dont worry
We'll seduce those trouble makers
with the price tag

Al I'm dropping a fortune
on that 8!

1st Developer Count me out

2nd Developer Me, too

4th Developer Over my head

3rd Developer 10 millions!

Al Peanut brittle

Mayor (*whispers to the dice & throwing*)

All together

8

Mayor You're number 1, Al
with that Fort
& the Watershed

Al Here's the note for the works

(handing the Mayor a paper)

we'll see now
who the tall tale makers are -
What's next, Mayor?

Mayor The Lynch Meadows on Farrington Ave

1st Developer 2 million

2nd Developer 1 million

Al (*throwing*)

Aha
a seven!

4th Developer 3 million

3rd Developer He's a connector

Al (picking dice & throwing)

a 5

1st Developer 2 million on a deuce

Al (*picking up & throwing*)

7!
You made it, Jocko!

3rd Developer OK
Mayor -
next?

Mayor The skirts of Dogtown

Al What do you mean,
skirt?

Mayor Just that
all open land
bordering on Indian Reservation

Al Wowie!

4th Developer Ideal of the real!

1st Developer For the skyscrapers

2nd Developer & Dogtown in the middle
Free!

3rd Developer An extra City of Stone
in Space –
our Central Park!

1st Developer A brain blast

Mayor Al
do I juggle these eyes?

Al like a fishtown wizard!

Mayor Now for the next knockout –
what offers do I have
for an Island Bostonia

1st Developer 50 million

Mayor (*whispering intimately to the dice*)
Raise the kitty, boys
This is the Queen of Choices
this is It –
with this purchase

everything changes
even the light of day
takes on the cat's meow!

1st Developer & the purring!
forevermore!

2nd Developer Can we carry it –
sure, we'll be the first
to build homes out of the granite
underground!
those holier than us
wont have a dog's fart
to lick on!

3rd Developer We'll be the pineapple of America!
Rough on the outside –
Kiss juicy on the inside!

Mayor O K Boys
ready for the Moon's prize

1st Developer 9 million on a nine!

2nd Developer Why dont you make it an even 10 –

1st Developer I'm an odds-man

Mayor You guys havent done
your homework

2nd Developer 1 billion on a 5

Al 11 million on a 7

Mayor Just keep in noodle-maker
we'll have to become like
German police hounds
teeth bared at all moments
no dog goes to sleep
not for one second
we wont even have time to meditate
day & night is one open eye
get it?

All Together Got it

Mayor It's all or nothing now (*throwing*)
3
anyone left out
want to get in

3rd Developer 9 billion on 6

2nd Developer I'm sweating cold
damp as a July dawn

3rd Developer & I've jumped into Rafe's Chasm
in a blizzard

Al we're jitterbugging
on the cutting sword

Mayor Speculation is our gambling Lady

1st Developer Yeah
a fickle pickle

(Helen enters in prison garb, watching them on the sideline)

Al

That ole Babson bastard
I'll bet he's drowning
in dungeon dew –
Imagine the unfucking dead
dictating from a gold coffin!
The fucking nerve of their ilk
with his dead fist on our Future
he's kept my blood in a seethe
by a rigor mortis
contract
how the hell did that renegade poet
put it

4th Developer

Ezrat Pound
that uneducated Pope of Literature
he hated money
because he never had enough of it
to use it wisely
that <u>usura</u> poem
about 'contra naturam' bullshit

Al

Babson's contra speculation
O he did damn well alive
but what's he fucking with the living for
throw those cat-eyes of tomorrow

1st Developer

Yeah

let's leap over this last hurdle!

Mayor (*tossing the dice in the air, catches them, shaking them behind his back, doing a dance of ecstacy sitting down*)

the far seeing eyes
in my money fingers
the only eyes that really see!

2nd Developer like the eyes of the dead
do

Al dead nature
we'll put the real eyes there
in all that black Mother Earth
we'll stick our upper eyes into her
as well as the eyes in our balls!

Mayor (*throwing the dice, as Helen with raised knife plunges it into Al's back, he cries out, as the Men are all eyes to the audience, Al drops dead*)

Helen (*letting the knife fall from her fingers*)

A bloody sight –
Drink, Mother Earth!
Your dark is full of light!

(*Curtain*)